NORFOLK
FOLK
TALES

NORFOLK
FOLK
TALES

HUGH LUPTON

The
History
Press

For my old friends from Keswick Mill, especially Tim
Brook, Michael Deason-Barrow, and in memory of
Jasmine Reeve

Back cover image courtesy of Tony Crossland.

First published 2013

The History Press
The Mill, Brimscombe Port
Stroud, Gloucestershire, GL5 2QG
www.thehistorypress.co.uk

British Library Cataloguing in Publication Data.
A catalogue record for this book is available from the British Library.

ISBN 978 0 7524 7942 2

Typesetting and origination by The History Press
Printed in Great Britain

CONTENTS

INTRODUCTION

Norfolk is steeped in story. Whether we are travelling along the coast, through the loam-rich farmlands, across the sandy brecklands, among the inland waterways of the broads, or over the marsh and fenlands to the west of the county; whether we are threading the Saxon and Medieval streets of Norwich, Kings Lynn or Thetford, stories are everywhere.

All the events that have happened in a place, all the geological and historical interactions, are held in the grain of a landscape. They are memories that lurk under the surface of the soil. Where they meet the human mind, they become something new. The Australian Aborigines would call this marriage of mind and land the 'Dreaming' of a place. It is not quite conscious. It is never altogether stable. It lies underneath the sunlit, familiar, waking world of the twenty-first century.

Like people everywhere (storytelling being a universal compulsion), the inhabitants of Norfolk have been part of this process. Over countless generations half-remembered histories, superstitions, beliefs, stories from elsewhere and leaps of imagination have been brought to bear on hills, wells, springs, sandbanks, trees, houses, stones, churches, bridges and much more besides. Landscape has precipitated story, and these ancient stories carry the voices of everyone who has told them.

I've been fascinated for a long time by this relationship between place, history and local imagination. The stories we tell ourselves about ourselves become part of who we are. They may be told to entertain, to warn, to elicit a chill shudder, to teach or to enlighten, but most of all they are told to reinforce a sense of belonging, of being alive in this place both now and in the past. Almost all of them are anchored to somewhere or something in the landscape that can still be seen today. As Dennis Tedlock has written: '… The sense of being in place exists at the same moment the story is being told … We have a mystery here, the story has to be connected up with the past and it has to be right here in front of us … An oral story is an action that's now, and that speaks of ancient things.'

These stories have moved in and out of print, but primarily their life has been on the tongue. They have been told and remembered, elaborated and embellished as part of a great spoken tradition. Many of the people who told them would not have been able to read or write. Like the weavers of Worsted cloth and Aylsham web, the people of Norfolk have always been skilled at spinning yarns, weaving tales and embroidering the truth.

Only one of the stories in this collection is a 'once upon a time' tale. The rest I would call 'legendary histories'. Some are from the remote past, some from the recent past. Some are fantastical. Some are matters of fact. All of them have a sense of life writ large, of the universal in the particular. All of them are imbued with the very particular topography, history and character of the County of Norfolk.

There's a tradition among the Gypsies and the Travellers that when a story is told, the ghosts of the people who told it before are standing behind the teller. As I've worked on these tales I've been very aware of other tellers: website contributors, twentieth-century folklorists, Victorian antiquarians, Medieval hagiographers, Anglo-Saxon and Roman historians … and most of all the countless, nameless, forgotten voices of the people.

Hugh Lupton, 2013

1

THE CALLOW PIT COFFER

The north door of a church is commonly known as the Devil's Door. According to Medieval belief the Devil resides in a child's soul until the moment of baptism. At the touch of holy water to the head he makes a swift exit through the north door. The association between door and Devil is doubly strong in the church of St Botolph at Limpenhoe. The latch of the north door is turned by an iron ring that was brought from the nearby church of St Edmund at Southwood when it fell into ruin. It is a ring that has a history.

In the enclosure maps there is a pit marked on the border between the parishes of Southwood and Moulton that is called 'The Callow Pit'. It was a pit that, according to local legend, held a treasure deep in its dark waters. Tradition is vague as to what the treasure might have been. It was certainly gold, but whether it was a smuggler's fortune, a viking's trophy, an Iceni hoard or an offering made to the spirits of the water in some deep forgotten past ... no one knows. Of one thing the good rectors of Southwood were certain: it was not Christian gold, and anyone meddling with it was putting his immortal soul in peril.

But times were hard in the years that followed the English Civil War. Chaos ruled and harvests failed. Many families struggled to keep their bellies filled.

In Southwood the story was the same, and two men of the village – two brothers – tired of seeing their children going to bed with their bellies aching with hunger, decided to try their luck at the Callow Pit. They shared a flagon of ale to give them courage. Their wives cautioned them:

'It's a wicked old place. There's them that's seen a headless horseman riding out of it. There's them that say it goes down and down to the very gates of Hell.'

But the two men paid them no heed. They cut a long straight pole and fitted an iron hook to the end of it. The two wives watched and shook their heads.

'Well, if you're set on going, you mind you keep your mouths shut … for whatever spooks reside in that place will be stirred by speech.'

The brothers shrugged; they went to the barn and fetched a long ladder.

'We know the pair of you well enough, we've heard you cuss and blaspheme when you've had a quart of ale. Well, you watch yourselves this night in that place and keep your tongues behind your teeth.'

The brothers grinned at each other. Each of them took a last swig from the flagon and they set off with pole and ladder into the black night.

There was just enough moon to see by. The path was familiar. They tramped in silence, one in front, the other behind, one carrying the top ends of the ladder and pole tucked under his arms, the other the bottom.

When they reached the Callow Pit, in its hollow of alders and stunted willows, it seemed to be an open mouth swallowing all light. The murky water gave no reflection; it drew the night into itself. They shuddered and set to work. They stretched the long ladder across the pit from bank to bank. They stepped out over the black water, rung by rung, one behind the other. The leading brother held the pole horizontally by its middle, like a tightrope walker. When they reached the centre they turned the pole upright so that the iron hook sent ripples across the murk. Then, slowly, hand over hand, they pushed it down and down into the water.

It was only when their hands and forearms clutching the top end of the pole were elbow deep in water that they felt the hook push into stiff, thick mud. Without a word, with the understanding that passes sometimes between brothers, they began to work the hook through the mud, twisting it, pushing, lifting, sliding it to left and right. They moved along the rungs of the ladder, poking the depths.

For half an hour they worked, until their hands were numb with the cold water. Then, suddenly, they felt the iron hook meet something hard. It was scraping the surface of something smooth and firm. They twisted the pole and the hook locked into something that held it fast. They began to pull. They felt a tremendous weight. Hand over hand, kneeling on the rungs, straining their backs and arms, they heaved the pole up and up from the water. The ladder creaked and groaned, but it held firm. Slowly, by the thin light of the moon, they saw what they had caught.

The hook had snagged onto an iron ring. As they pulled it out of the black pit, they saw that it was attached to an iron lid, red and crusted with rust. Then, slowly a huge iron coffer emerged from the water, fastened with a lock of burnished brass. It was filled with something heavy that slid this way and that. The two brothers curled their fingers under the coffer and lifted. They set it across the ladder. There was a place where the lid had rusted clean away. Inside, there was no mistaking the yellow glint of golden coins catching the moonlight. The brothers could feel each other's grins, even if they couldn't see them. They threaded the pole through the iron ring. One stood behind, one in front. They heaved the pole onto their shoulders and set off, rung by rung, back to the bank of the Callow Pit, the coffer swinging between them.

When the first brother had set foot on firm ground he could contain himself no longer. He turned and shouted over his shoulder:

'We've got it safe now, by Jesus Christ and all the Saints, and damn me if Old Nick shall ever take it from us!'

No sooner were the words spoken than a reek of yellow sulphur began to seethe and bubble from the pit. The brothers coughed and spluttered. They scrambled up the bank. Behind them there was a splash. They turned their heads and saw an enormous black hand rising from the murk. It turned from side to side as though it had an eye in its palm, then it lunged. A hand, a wrist, a forearm, an elbow … a whole arm emerged as quick as the crack of a whip. It lunged towards them. The black fingers curled around the coffer and pulled it back towards the water. The second brother flattened himself against the mud. The iron ring slid along the pole and caught once again in the hook. The two brothers seized the pole and pulled with all their strength. A terrible tug of war ensued. The brothers dug their heels into the willow roots and pulled one way, the black arm pulled the other.

Then came a crack, a sudden sharp clanking crack as the iron ring broke from the rusty lid of the coffer. The brothers fell backwards against the bank. When they sat up, the black hand had vanished, and all that was left of the coffer was a trail of bubbles breaking the surface of the Callow Pit.

And caught on the hook at the end of the pole, the heavy iron ring was swinging and dangling.

When they got home their wives were waiting for them with their hands on their hips. They looked at the iron ring and shook their heads.

'I don't suppose you broke silence and cussed, did ye?'

The brothers' shut mouths were all the answer they needed.

They took the ring to the parson who fixed it to the door of Southwood Church, and there it hung until 1881 when it was taken to Limpenhoe and hung from the door there, the north door of course, the Devil's Door.

2

THE POTTER
HEIGHAM DRUMMER

The 9th (East Norfolk) Regiment of the Foot were also known as the 'Holy Boys'. This was because the regiment's badge, the image of Britannia, was mistaken by the Spanish and Portuguese allies during the Peninsular War for the Virgin Mary.

After serving with distinction in Spain, the regiment was sent to Canada in 1814 to prevent the United States' threatened invasion (America seeing herself as being in sympathy with France as a sister republic).

Between the Spanish and Canadian campaigns of the Napoleonic wars, there was a brief lull when the soldiers of the regiment were granted furlough or leave. Many of them returned to their villages in Norfolk.

One of them was a drummer from Potter Heigham. He'd been sold into the regiment by his pauper father when he was ten years old. He was now sixteen. He came home to find that his father was dead and his mother had remarried. There was no home for him to return to. But six years in the army had taught him resourcefulness. With his soldier's wage he bought an old canvas sail and made himself a tent on a piece of common land outside the village. Although it was mid-winter, he kept himself snug with a blazing fire. Every morning he would saunter into the village in his red military jacket with its shining buttons, and buy bread and tobacco.

The villagers recognised him.

'Old Jess Dyble's boy is back I see.'

'Yip, an' squatting on the common like a gypsy.'

There was something about the lad that they fought shy of. It wasn't just that he was the son of a pauper; it was something more dangerous than that. He'd seen more in his six years away from home than they'd seen in their lifetimes. It was clear in his face that had been tanned brown by the Spanish sun, and bore on its cheek a long scar. It was in his eyes too, that seemed to hold secrets they didn't want to enquire into. It was as though the war had left the boy both wounded and fearless.

For the girls of the village, it was a different story. That combination of wounded and fearless was a potent brew. They watched him cooking over his fire, self-composed and contented, whistling to himself. They watched him leaning over the bridge by the boatyards, smoking his pipe and spitting into the river. They watched his red jacket among the smocks and grey fustian overcoats of the village boys. Every one of the girls was smitten, but it was Eliza Rust, the prettiest and boldest of them all, who went up to him first.

'Are you one of the Holy Boys?'

He smiled at her.

'I am, Lizzie ...'

She gasped.

'How did you know my name?'

'Because I remember you from before I marched away. A soldier never forgets a pretty face. Don't you remember me, Nathan Dyble ... little Natty?'

She looked into his eyes.

'So you are – I'd clean forgot you. You was sold into the army and your father drank away the shilling the night you was took.'

'That'd be me. Now, what would you say to a ribbon for that hat of yours?'

And so it was that Nathan Dyble walked Lizzie Rust to the village shop, pulled out his purse and bought her a ribbon that matched his jacket. The next day he walked her along the towpath by the river. The next day he borrowed a boat and rowed her out onto the broad.

It was there that her father saw them, talking and laughing and looking into each other's faces like a couple of sweethearts. As soon as she came home, he called her: 'Eliza, you come here.'

He was standing by the fire, trembling with rage.

'You leave that boy alone. He ain't no good. He ain't got a roof over his head ... and we all know what stock he come from. A redcoat on furlough has only one thing on his mind ... and no daughter of mine will be a soldier's whore. You'll not see him again, do you understand, not never!'

But her father was too late; poor Lizzie was completely smitten by Nathan Dyble, and Nathan had no intention of giving up on her. When one of Lizzie's friends came to his tent on the Common and said: 'Lizzie Rust's been warned off you, and her Dad says you and she are through for good and all.' Nathan seized her by the hand and whispered: 'You tell Lizzie Rust this: if she loves me as I love her, then she's to wait for me at Swim Coots tomorrow night. If she don't come, then I'll up sticks and bid farewell to Potter Heigham, and she'll never see me no more.'

That night was bitterly cold; in the morning there was a skin of ice on Hickling Broad that thickened with every hour that passed. By the time the sun set, it was strong enough to take a man's weight.

Lizzie Rust lay in bed, waiting for her parents' breathing on the other side of the thin partition wall to grow steady and even. When she was sure they were asleep, she slipped downstairs. She had hidden warm clothes beneath the wooden settle. She dressed herself and pulled a thick coat over her woollen clothes. She pulled back the bolt and slipped out of the cottage. It was frosty, and there was a strong moon. The world was black and white and silver. The grass crunched beneath her feet. She made her way along the lanes that ran beside the icy marshes to Swim Coots. She held herself against the bitter cold, looking out across the smooth wide expanse of the frozen broad. There was no sound; no sign of life. She waited and waited.

And then, suddenly, from the middle of the broad, there came a sound. It was the rattling and the rolling of a military drum, the crisp tattoo of a military parade. And then she saw him. He was skating towards her across the frozen lake in the full uniform of the Ninth Regiment of Foot, every button burnished in the moonlight, playing his drum as though a thousand men were marching to its rhythm. As he approached her, he lifted his drum-sticks to his forehead and crossed them. He stepped nimbly onto the frozen ground, unfastened his skates and took her in his arms. His face was flushed, and his body was warm from the exertion. She folded herself against him. Their mouths met. He unbuttoned her coat and threw it down onto the white grass. And there, beneath the clear winter moon, they lay down together, and all of her father's worst fears were realised in an hour of unbridled happiness.

When they parted he whispered: 'Tomorrow?'

And she replied: 'Tomorrow.'

Night after night they met at Swim Coots. Night after night, he came skating across the broad with the tan-tan-tarra of his regimental drum. Night after night, they pitted their warmth against the bitter February chill.

But then one night she saw him coming towards her across the ice. He was beating his sticks against the skin of his drum but there was no sound. He stepped onto the ground and took her into his arms. She found herself shuddering at his touch: 'My love ... you are so cold.'

Without saying a word he unbuttoned her coat. She wriggled out of it and dropped it onto the ground. She seized his hand to draw him down ... but her fingers closed around water. Her hand was wet with ice-cold water and where he had been standing there was nothing. Nobody. She was quite alone.

Suddenly she was filled with a chill terror.

'Nathan!'

She ran out onto the ice, but it creaked and groaned and heaved under her weight so that she was forced to return to the edge of the broad. She ran along the edge of the broad, but thick cloud had covered the moon and she could see nothing. She made her way back to the village, not daring to say a word, knowing that if her father guessed the truth he would throw her out of house and home. She slipped through the door and climbed the stairs to bed. When she woke, a cold rain was battering the window-panes. She told her mother that she was feeling indisposed and stayed beneath the bedclothes. She slept fitfully through the day, and as it grew dark outside she came downstairs to the kitchen fire. Her father was warming his feet at the hearth. He looked up at her.

'Well Lizzie, it's just as well you done as I told you and didn't go breaking your heart over poor Jess Dyble's son.'

Lizzie paled.

'Why's that?'

'They've just fished him out of the broad, drowned as a rat. He'd gone through the ice they reckon ... though why he should have been dressed in the full uniform of the Holy Boys is a mystery no one can unravel ... and if he hadn't been strapped to that drum of his they reckon he'd have sunk to the bottom ... what's the matter Lizzie ...'

'She ain't well, poor child', said Lizzie's mother, 'Now you get back upstairs to bed, my sweet, and I'll bring you up a bowl of gruel.'

༄

It is said that Nathan Dyble's ghost is still seen on Hickling Broad, but only in winter when the ice is beginning to melt. An old wherryman, recorded in 1906, put it this way: 'The folks ha' a notion that th' Hickling drummer lad go skaten' round Swim Cutes, a-beaten o' his drum ter show that th' ice ain't safe.'

And if you want to see a drum of the 9th Regiment of Foot, then go to the Royal Norfolk Regimental Museum in Norwich Castle where there's one on display.

3

THE PLOUGHMAN
AND THE PHARISEES

Three of the greatest traditional singers recorded during the folk-music revival of the 1950s, '60s and '70s have come from Norfolk: Walter Pardon, a carpenter from Knapton; Harry Cox, a farm labourer from Catfield; and Sam Larner, a fisherman from Winterton. All three had huge repertoires of song, much of which is available to us still thanks to the recordings made by folksong collectors over the years.

The cottage in Bulmer Lane, Winterton, where Sam Larner lived and died is marked by a blue plaque. He was the most exuberant of the three. He first went to sea when he was eight, signed on as a cabin boy aboard a sailing lugger when he was twelve, and spent most of his working life on steam drifters, following the shoals of herring.

The singer Martin Carthy remembers hearing him sing in 1959. 'His impact was immediate and electrifying. This was a man in command, utterly accustomed to performing. He pointed at his audience, he teased them, he pulled words out of the air ... I took away an impression of someone utterly at home with what he was doing, for whom every song was personal ... and 'The Lofty Tall Ship' ... with its endless variations, was as exotic as anything I had ever heard.'

Sam, although he never worked the land, would almost certainly have known the Winterton story of the Ploughman and the Pharisees, though it is to the reminiscences of Harry Cox that we need to go in order to get a sense of the rural hardship that is the backdrop to the story: 'Used to eat turnips sometimes – had to get what you could – I have been hungry - well a labourer, he never got only ten shillings a week – that's all we got – I've seen more dinner-times than I've had dinners. When I first began I got half a crown a week. It was a long long while afore I got very much more – I got a little better off as I got older – not much. You paid seven shillings for your board, and then you had the rest. Lot of them used to wear old second-hand slops we called them – jompers. That they did – and old tanned ones.'

Sam Larner would have been eighteen when this story was published in the Folklore Journal in 1896. It was told by a Winterton woman called Mrs Goodale. She had heard it from her grandmother.

There were hard times once, and terrible hard times. Food was dear, wages were low and families were large:

> Provisions you buy at a shop it is true
> But if you've no money there's none there for you,
> So what's a poor man and his family to do?
> And it's O, the hard times of Old England
> In Old England very hard times.

In Winterton there lived a farm labourer. His breakfast had been crust and cold water, and that's no ballast for a good day's ploughing. As he pulled on his boots to go to work he said to his wife: 'I wish one of them Pharisees would give me a bit of luck.'

That morning he was set to ploughing his master's 11-acre field. When the horses had been harnessed and led to the field, he got between the stilts of the plough.

'Whoaaa!'

As the horses moved forwards, the blade of the plough sliced and turned the earth. All morning he followed the plough. And then, suddenly, he saw something shining in the turned earth. He stopped the horses, reached down and picked it up. It was the size and shape of a silver shilling ... but the head on it was of no king

or queen he'd heard tell of. And the tail-side showed what seemed
to be a lean steed and a turning wheel.

'Well I'll be …'

It was as bright as a new-minted coin, as bright as a full moon.
He dropped it into his pocket.

'Where there was one – may there be more.'

He shook the reins and carried on working.

At the end of the day, he went home and put the coin on the
table. He said to his wife: 'Get you down to the shop and buy
some meat for supper.'

She picked up the coin between finger and thumb and turned
it over. She gave her husband a quizzical look but asked no
questions.

'As long as Old Brown's behind the counter, and not his
daughter, I reckon it'll pass muster as the King's coin.'

Luckily it was Old Brown, whose eyes were fading, behind the
shop's counter. That evening their children went to bed with their
bellies full. When they were asleep, the ploughman and his wife
raised their mugs of beer: 'Here's to the bee that stung Adam's arse
and set the world a-joggin'.'

The next day, the plough turned up two silver shillings.

'Where there were two – may there be plenty.'

The next day there were four.

The next day there were eight.

Now the ploughman and his wife may have had no schooling,
but they both had a head for numbers.

'If that takes a day to plough an acre, then I reckon you'll be
ploughing that field for eleven days.'

'I will, and if there's one coin on day one, two on day two, four
on day three and eight on day four …'

'Then there'll be sixteen on day five, thirty-two on day six,
sixty-four on day seven, 128 on day eight, 256 on day nine …'

The ploughman whistled between his teeth.

'And more'n a thousand on the last day … and you know, and I
know, what must and must not be spoken of.'

His wife nodded and they called the children to their supper.

Both of them knew, as all people in those days knew, that any gift from the Pharisees, or the Fair People, must not be explained or given thanks for. One word and it would disappear from sight.

The next morning, as her husband was working, the ploughman's wife went to the miller to buy flour for her baking. When her bag had been filled she pulled a silver shilling from her purse and handed it across.

The miller's eyes were as sharp as gimlets.

'Where did this come from?'

'It's just a shilling coin.'

'Not like any I've seen before, give me another.'

She gave him another from her purse.

'It's just the same … and I'll not take it.'

He seized the bag and tipped the flour back into his sack.

'Judas Iscariot was paid with forty pieces of silver, and I reckon you've got two of them.'

The woman had no choice but to go home empty-handed. That evening, sure enough, the ploughman came home with sixteen silver shillings. They put the money into a little wooden box and kept it under their straw mattress.

The next day she went to the village shop in Winterton. Old Brown's daughter was behind the counter. When she'd been paid she held the coin to the light.

'Is this ducats or dollars? It ain't the King's money.'

'It's just a shilling, same as any other.'

'Well, I'll not take it.'

Once again the ploughman's wife went home with nothing. And that night the family sat down to a supper as thin as any they'd known before the coins appeared. When the children were asleep, they fetched the box from under the bed.

'Thirty-two today … let's make a tally. Maybe you could take them to London and swap them for coins of the realm.'

They lit a candle and set to counting up the money. As they were piling the glistening coins one on top of another, there came a sudden knock at the door. The ploughman got to his feet. He lifted the latch and opened the door. The miller, Old

Brown, his daughter, the parson and the farmer who owned the 11-acre field were all standing outside. The farmer spoke: 'We've been watching you through the window and we'd like you to explain to us where this new-found money is coming from.'

The ploughman shook his head: 'I ain't telling.'

Then the parson turned to the ploughman's wife: 'Maybe you could shed some light on the matter.'

She shrugged her shoulders and held her tongue.

'Well then,' said the farmer, 'a nothing of an answer shall be rewarded with a nothing of a job. I'll thank you not to show your face in my yard again.'

And then Old Brown's shrill wavering voice came out of the shadows: 'And there's not a tradesman in Norfolk will take your god-forsaken money – I'll see to that.'

The ploughman closed the door. Surely the silver money was worth something somewhere? But though he trudged far and wide, nobody would take it. Soon he was destitute, without a job or money and his children were crying with hunger.

Some nights later, he and his wife were sitting and shivering at the table when there came a knocking again. This time, the farmer was standing alone on the doorstep.

'I'll give you one last chance. Tell me the truth and you can have your job back.'

The ploughman had no choice. He told his story from beginning to end, and as he did so, a strange whispering, rustling sound filled the air like a wind, though not so much as a leaf stirred. The farmer listened and stroked his chin. When the tale was finished he said: 'Alright then. Six o'clock tomorrow morning at the threshing barn, and don't be late.'

As soon as he was gone, the ploughman and his wife ran to the bed, and reached under the mattress. The box was still there, but when they opened the lid it was as empty as a broken promise.

And he never found another silver shilling as long as he drew breath, though he ploughed the 11-acre field every autumn for fifty long years.

And it's O the hard times of old England
In old England very hard times.

But hard times sometimes have unexpected silver linings. If it hadn't been for the great depression of the 1930s, Sam Larner wouldn't have been laid off the fishing fleet, and he wouldn't have brought his great repertoire of songs, mostly learned at sea, to a new audience.

If it hadn't been for the depression, Walter Pardon wouldn't have sat down with his uncle Billy Gee: 'When times were bad he'd be laid off … we'd sit of an afternoon in one of the sheds. He'd keep a bottle of something or other under the floorboards and he'd get that out and we'd sit there, the two of us, him singing and me listening. And that's how I got most of my songs.'

And Harry Cox, if times hadn't been hard, would maybe have had other diversions: 'Sometimes I done seven months at a stretch, Sundays and all, no rest, never had a holiday – nowhere to go. All we used to do then of a night … we used to get beside the old fire … and we had a song or two to pass the time. We had to cheer ourselves up. That was all the frolic we had.'

Out of those hard times came what Walter called a 'bright golden store' of songs. Worth nothing, perhaps, in the gimlet-eyed marketplace, but a treasure nonetheless – every bit as precious as the Snettisham hoard.

THE THREE UNGRATEFUL SONS

In Winterton, there once lived a wealthy merchant. He had lived a long and prosperous life, but when he reached his dotage he decided to divide all his wealth between his three sons. The condition was that each of them should look after him, one this week, one the next, taking it in turns, for whatever years were left to him.

As soon as the money had been divided his sons lost interest in the poor old man. They fed him on scraps. They made him sleep on a pile of rags by an unlit fire. They ignored him when he spoke to them. It was the same in each household.

The old man had a friend who was a lawyer in Yarmouth. One day, he paid him a visit and told his story. The lawyer listened and shook his head.

'All your wealth and property is 'titled to them. Nothing I could do would bring it back.'

'Then what am I to do? I'll starve to death if you can't help me.'

The lawyer stroked his chin and pondered.

'There's only one solution.'

'Tell me!'

'Well, you've always been a good friend to me, and now I shall be the same to you.'

He went to the safe in the corner of the room. He unlocked it, and returned with an iron-bound chest. He opened it. It was full to the brim with golden sovereigns.

'Here are a thousand sovereigns. I will lend them to you for three weeks. Tell your sons that you've brought them from a safe hiding place. When you stay with each in turn you must make a great show of counting the money into golden piles. I've a mind you'll find those mean-spirited boys of yours will quickly change their tune.'

The old man thanked his friend with all his heart. He took the money and did as he'd been advised. He stayed in the first son's house. As soon as his supper of dry bread was eaten, he fetched the chest and unfastened it. With a great chinking and clinking he began to count the money. The sound of coins soon drew his son.

'Where did that come from?'

'Oh, it's just a trifle I've been keeping to one side.'

Suddenly, he found he was being ushered into a warm parlour with a blazing fire. A mutton pie and a flagon of ale was set before him. That night he slept on a feather bed, between sheets of white linen … with the locked chest safely under the bedclothes beside him.

It was the same story in the other two households. On the fourth week he began the circuit again. This time he had no gold. His eldest son asked: 'Where's that chest of gold you brought with you last time?'

'Oh that, well, it's put safely back where it came from … with its companions.'

'And what's to become of it all?'

'It'll be for the son that truly loved me.'

For years the old man was treated as an honoured guest by his three sons.

When he was a hundred years old, he felt the cold hand of death closing around his heart. The three sons sat at his bedside and watched him receive the last rites. The old man's breath became fainter and fainter. At last they could bear it no longer.

'Well, Father, which one of us shall inherit your gold?'

He opened one eye and looked at their eager, greedy faces.

'He who truly loved me shall have it all, every coin.'

The brothers looked at one another and leaned forwards.

'Who's that?'

But the old man's eyes were fixed on the ceiling, his hands were limp on the bed, and his mouth was twisted into a strange, inscrutable smile.

THE LIE OF THE LAND
~ HILLS, MOUNDS AND
HIDDEN TREASURES

Norfolk rests on a floor of chalk. For 70 million years, beneath a forgotten ocean, microscopic sea creatures worked on the calcium that had been carried by ancient rivers, and made chalk. It took 30,000 years for 1 ft of chalk to form. At the same time, the silicon from sponges that grew on that ancient seabed was compacted into hard nuggets of flint.

Then the ice ages came. Huge plates of ice, hundreds of yards thick, accumulated over the chalk. The ground was smoothened by relentless, grinding acres of ice. And when the glaciers melted, their streams of molten ice deposited beds of gravel and sand, sheets of earth, blankets of boulder-clay. The gently undulating flatlands of Norfolk had been given form.

In a low-lying landscape a hill is an event.

It's said that the Devil once took the notion to take a load of gravel and earth from where Neatishead Hall Farm is today. The pit that he dug can still be seen. He loaded the earth into his wheelbarrow and started for home. But as he was pushing it through Irstead, the wheel caught in a dip of land, the barrow 'bunked' and the spilt soil formed Bunker's Hill. The Devil cursed. A quarter of his load was gone. Then he spilt some more on the banks of the River Ant. That part of the river, called 'The Shoals', has been gravelly ever since. The Devil swore. His barrow was half empty. He carried on pushing. At Ludham he caught his hoof, tipped the barrow and spilled two more piles – two more hills that are now known as the Great Reedham and the Little Reedham. The Devil ground his teeth. The load was almost gone. Then, he lost his grip on the handles, the barrow turned over, and the last of the gravel was tipped out. The Devil rolled his red eyes, threw back his head and bellowed 'How?'

And so it was that How Hill came into being and found its name. Seeing that his labours were wasted, the Devil stamped his hoof on the ground in fury; the earth opened and swallowed him and his wheelbarrow.

On another occasion the Devil decided to make the Devil's Dyke, a 'holloway' that runs north-south across Garboldisham and East Harling heaths. He made it by dragging one of his hooves along the ground. When he had finished, he scraped the dirt from his hoof. It fell to the ground at Thetford and formed the mound at Castle Hill. A hollow that fills with water to the north-east of Castle Hill is known as the Devil's Hole – anyone who walks round it seven times at midnight will catch a glimpse of him.

Cromer Bay, notoriously difficult to navigate, is sometimes known as The Devil's Throat because it's always open and eager to swallow unwitting sailors, and bring them to their doom.

When the first Christians came to Anglo-Saxon England, they were eager to demonise the old gods. Odin (or Woden) had been the 'Allfather', the most powerful of the Saxon/Viking pantheon. He was quickly identified with the Devil. Many Devil stories carry traces of older deities. Odin was also known as Grim – from the Norse 'Grimr' meaning 'Masked One'. As Grim he gave his name to one of the most famous ancient sites in Norfolk.

A couple of miles east of Brandon there are the hollowed traces of 366 flint mines. They were dug during the Neolithic period – one of the oldest industrial sites in the world – and tools made from their prime-quality flint have been found across Britain and Europe. When the Saxons came and found the old workings with their tunnels going down deep into the ground, it made perfect sense to call the place Grim's Graves. One of Odin's roles was, after all, to lead the dead to Niflheim, the realm far below that is presided over by the goddess Hel.

Norfolk is littered with round barrows. Inevitably, they accrue local names. One of them has become associated with one of Norfolk's most renowned daughters.

In Garboldisham, between Home Covert and the Devil's Dyke there is a large round barrow known as Soldier's Hill. It is supposed to be the burial place of Boadicea. Several other places have made the same claim (including Platform A at Kings Cross Station), but Soldier's Hill makes the most convincing case. Historians are (mostly) in agreement that the Iceni had their headquarters in the Thetford area. It would have been from here that the massed army of the Iceni tribes rode out to sack Colchester, London and Verulanium (now known as St Albans), and finally met their match when they were confronted by the Roman General Suetonius somewhere near Nuneaton. Not much is known of Boadicea. It is not clear whether her revolt was to avenge the rape of her daughters and the seizing of her lands by the Imperial Procurator Catus, or whether it was a response to the destruction of the sacred groves and the annihilation of the Druidic priesthood on Anglesey.

The Roman historian Cassius Dio (writing more than 100 years later) described her: 'She was very tall, in appearance terrifying, in the glance of her eye most fierce, and her voice was harsh; a great mass of the tawniest hair fell to her hips; around her neck she wore a large golden necklace; and she wore a tunic of diverse colours over which a thick mantle was fastened with a brooch.' The only first-hand account we have of her is from the Roman historian Tacitus, who describes her, on the eve of her final battle, releasing a hare between the two armies and watching the course it followed. This would suggest that she was as much a priestess as queen. Whether the zigzagging of the hare gave any hint of the disaster that was to follow, history doesn't relate. The Celts were slaughtered and the Romans imposed an iron rule. According to Tacitus, 80,000 Britons were killed. Boadicea, it is said, seeing the devastation, took poison and died. And where else would the exhausted, rag-tag survivors of the battle have carried her body, but home to the heartland of her broken kingdom?

The Peddars Way, the straight Roman road that runs across Norfolk from Knettishall to Holme was built by slave labour to make sure there would be no further trouble. Its fosses and aggers are still visible. The garrison town at Caistor St Edmunds, mockingly called 'Venta Icenorum' (Market-town of the Iceni) was another military base. Its ragged flint walls can still be seen above the fields, a huge square of masonry redolent of Roman military power.

Norfolk soil revealed one of its greatest mysteries in 1948. A ploughman in Snettisham 'deep ploughing' a field on Ken Hill discovered a piece of shining metal. He showed it to the foreman: 'I reckon that's part of an old brass bedstead.'

He flung it to the edge of the field.

A passer-by noticed it and took it to the Norwich museum, where it was identified as being part of a golden torque. The field was excavated and revealed pits containing a hoard of more than 170 torques, seventy-five of them complete, many of them exquisite in their workmanship. There were also coins and ingots of gold, silver and iron. The 20-acre site was surrounded by a ditched enclosure. The treasure was dated to 70 BC, four generations before Boadicea, when Iceni power and prestige would have been at its height. The hoard almost certainly represents the royal treasury of the ruling house of the Iceni, the richest Iron Age treasure ever found in Britain ... though why it was buried, no one knows.

Boadicea is not the only monarch buried under a Norfolk hill.

It's said that the city of Norwich was founded by a certain King Gurgunt, and that he is buried deep under the hill on which Norwich Castle stands. When Queen Elizabeth I made her royal progress through Norwich in 1578, she was met by sixty of the most handsome men of the city, followed by 'one which represented King Gurgunt, sometyme King of England, which buylded the castle of Norwich ... and layde the foundation of the citie'. King Gurgunt was followed by three henchmen carrying his helmet, shield and staff. He stepped forward to speak, but a sudden shower of rain made the Queen hurry for shelter and the words were never uttered.

The legend was almost certainly invented to please the Queen. The Tudors liked anything that linked their rule to a line of ancient British kings. Gurgunt had been salvaged from Geoffrey of Monmouth's *History of the Kings of Britain*.

But these stories, once invented, take on a life of their own. By the nineteenth century Gurgunt was not dead, but like Arthur and Charlemagne, he was merely sleeping, waiting for Norfolk's hour of need when he will wake up and ride out to right all wrongs. So, even to this day, he sits and snores on his throne, deep inside Castle Hill. He's fully armed, his sword is in his hand, and his gold and silver treasures are scattered about him, and (as Walter Rye puts it) he's 'ready for all contingencies'.

6

HOLY WELLS
AND HOLY RELICS

ST WALSTAN

The shrine to St Walstan at Bawburgh church has almost
disappeared, but a pilgrim offering-box from the twelfth century
survives. It is curiously phallic in shape, and gives a clue to the
pre-Christian origins of the cult of the patron saint of stockmen
and husbandmen.

The legend tells us that Walstan was the son of Benedict and Blide. He was born during the reign of Ethelred the Unready. He was of noble birth, but renounced his inheritance and chose to work as a farm labourer in Taverham. He became noted for his humility and kindness, often giving away his food and possessions to those in greater need. When he wasn't working, he was praying. His employer was so impressed that he offered to make Walstan his heir, but Walstan refused. He gestured to a cow that was in calf and said: 'Give me instead the burden of that cow.'

The farmer agreed. In time, the cow was delivered of two snow-white bull calves. Walstan looked after them and they thrived under his care.

One day, while Walstan was ploughing, he heard angels singing and the bells of paradise ringing. He shouted to a fellow ploughman: 'Do you hear that?'

But the ploughman could hear nothing until he placed his foot upon Walstan's, when suddenly the air was bright with heavenly music.

As Walstan listened, he understood that the angels were singing of the day of his death. When the day came, he told his master that he wanted to be given the last rites in the fields, so that all plants and creatures could be blessed by him. He also asked that his body should be laid on a cart drawn by the two white bulls. The place where they halted would be his final resting place. All was done as he had asked. But the priest forgot to bring water to mix with wine for the final sacrament. Walstan whispered a prayer and a spring burst out of the ground (close to where Taverham church now stands). After the last rites had been administered, his lifeless body was laid on the cart, and the two white bulls set off at a trot. They made their way through Costessey Woods. They crossed the River Wensum as though it was dry land, and the wheel tracks can still sometimes be seen on the surface of the water. They rested at what is now Costessey Park where another sacred well sprang up. Finally, they reached the foot of the hillock upon which Bawburgh church now stands. The two bulls urinated and a third well appeared. At the top of the hillock they stopped, and wouldn't move until the body had been buried.

Over the grave a shrine was built, and so many miracles took place that pilgrims flocked to Bawburgh. By the thirteenth century, a church had been built to house the shrine; it supported six chantry priests and a vicar.

But it was farmers and labourers who most cherished St Walstan. They would come once a year on the 30 May to obtain blessings for themselves and their beasts. And long after the Reformation, well into the nineteenth century, farm labourers would gather mosses and water from the three holy wells, convinced of their curative powers.

Beneath the Christian veneer, the story of St Walstan has ancient associations. His mother's name is almost certainly a corruption of Bride or Brigit, the Celtic goddess of fertility, cattle and crops, and latterly a Christian saint associated with milk-yield and midwifery. His father's name means 'blessed' but could also be derived from the Middle English 'bean-dic' or 'bean-ditch'. Bulls were sacred to the Celts, and white ones were associated with the 'Otherworld'. In the Germanic tradition, there was a fertility goddess called Nerthus whose image was carried in a cart drawn by bulls.

The legend is clearly the relic of a fertility cult. Under a veneer of Christian propriety the farmers of Norfolk could continue an ancient propitiation. And the pilgrim's offering box in Bawburgh church gives us a clue to the ancient potency of St Walstan.

The saint's image can be seen in several Norfolk rood-screens. He's at Barnham Broom church, with his two oxen; at Ludham with a scythe; and at Sparham with both.

Saint Witburgha

In the churchyard of St Nicholas church in East Dereham, where the ground slopes away beneath the west wall, is St Witburgha's well.

Saint Witburgha was one of the four sainted daughters of King Ana, who ruled East Anglia between 637 and 654. The others were St Etheldreda, St Ethelburgha and St Sexburgha.

She is said to have lived as a hermit on her father's summer estate at Holkham. The church of St Witburgha, on a mound in the grounds of Holkham Hall, is purportedly built on the site of her hermitage.

Later in life she moved southwards to East Dereham, where she founded a monastery, and gathered around her a group of female companions. While they were building the monastery, a time of terrible dearth and famine afflicted East Anglia. Harvests failed and cattle sickened. Witburgha and her acolytes would have died of starvation, had she not prayed for divine assistance. No sooner had she uttered her prayer than two deer, does with swollen udders, stepped out of the woodland that surrounded the monastery. They offered their teats to the women, who knelt down and suckled gratefully. Day after day the deer returned and the women's lives were saved.

But there was a town reeve in Dereham who had glimpsed the miraculous feeding of the women. He was consumed with jealousy that their bellies should be filled when everyone else's were hollow. He set his hunting dogs on the two deer. They bounded away. He blew his horn and urged the dogs on. He whipped his horse to a gallop (as can be seen on the town sign), but didn't notice an overhanging branch. He struck his head and broke his neck. The next day the deer shyly returned and fed the women as before.

When Witburgha died, her body was buried in the churchyard at Dereham. But in 974 the abbot of Ely, Brithnoth, decided that he wanted the relics of St Witburgha for his monastery in Ely. He already had the remains of two of her sisters, and with hers, the sanctity of the monastery would be guaranteed.

He travelled along creeks and over land with a large company of monks. They carried hampers filled with bread, meat, cheese and honey-cakes, and barrels of strong ale. When they reached Dereham they invited the townspeople to a feast. When they had eaten their fill, and washed their meal down with copious quantities of ale, the people of Dereham had no choice but to lie down and sleep.

Brithnoth and his monks wasted no time. With spades they dug up the body of St Witburgha. To their amazement she was uncorrupted after 300 years in her grave. Her body was laid in a new coffin, and the monks hurried to Brandon where a boat was waiting to carry them to the Isle of Ely. They were only just in time. The people of Dereham woke up from their drunken slumbers and found that their saint had been stolen. They set off in pursuit, and reached Brandon just as the monks' boat was pulling away from the quayside. There was a tumult of outraged shouting, and a rain of arrows fell upon the monks, but Brithnoth urged them to keep pulling at their oars and they made good their escape.

When the people of Dereham returned to the robbed grave, they found that it had filled with water. A spring had burst out of the ground, and it was found to have healing powers. Their saint had not forgotten them.

Meanwhile, the body of St Withburgha was placed alongside her sisters, St Etheldreda and St Sexburgha. When the new cathedral at Ely had been completed in 1106, the three sister-saints were to be moved to a new resting place in front of the high altar. Their caskets were opened. St Sexburgha was found to be only bones; the body of St Etheldreda was still intact but stiff with rigor mortis. But the body of St Witburgha was not only uncorrupted, but her limbs were still flexible. One of the monks proved it by lifting and moving her hands, arms and feet.

She can be seen on two rood screens: at Barnham Broom with a doe, and at St Andrews, North Burlingham, with two does.

LADY RICHELDIS

There are two wells that can be visited in Walsingham. One is in the grounds of the ruined Augustinian abbey; the other is in the Anglican shrine that was built over an ancient well in 1931. Both are holy wells, though which can claim to be the original Mary's Well is not known. But the choice between two wells is embedded in the Walsingham legend.

It's said that during the reign of Edward the Confessor, there lived, in the town of Walsingham, a devout widow called Lady Richeldis. She was granted three visions. Three times in her sleep she was visited by the Virgin Mary. In her dream, the Virgin took Lady Richeldis by the hand and led her over land and sea to the Holy House in Nazareth, the place where she had been visited by the Angel Gabriel and told that she was to conceive a son who 'shall be called the son of God'. The Virgin Mary turned to Lady Richeldis and gestured to the Holy House: 'You must build another like this, at Walsingham, unto my laud and singular honour so that all who come seeking me shall find succour.'

On three successive nights Lady Richeldis had the same dream, and by the time she woke from the third dream, she had measured in her mind the length, breadth and height of the Holy House.

She employed some local builders and they set out with ropes, hammers, saws, chisels, nails, pegs and timbers to build the Holy House. But where was it to be built? It was a bright May morning and the grass was wet with dew, but there were two places, each beside a well, where the grass was 'as dry as the fleece of Gideon'. They were measured and found to be exactly the length and breadth of the Holy House. This was clearly a sign, but still there was a dilemma. Which of the two should Lady Richeldis choose? She decided on one and the builders set to work.

All day they laboured, but nothing would join or hold. No beam or lintel would stay level. Wooden pegs popped out of their holes. Even the most skilled craftsmen could only make a bodged job of it. Lady Richeldis told them to lay down their tools and go home. Then she knelt and prayed, trusting that the Virgin would reveal her true intent. All night she prayed and the workmen slept.

And as she prayed, the Virgin Mary, with a great host of angels carrying ropes, hammers, saws, chisels, nails and pegs descended from the heavens. They lifted up the timbers of the Holy House and set them down beside the other well. They rebuilt the Holy House with such skill and grace that when the builders found it the next morning, they dropped to their knees in amazement. Its construction was beyond the measure of their minds.

And so, as the Holy Lands were overwhelmed by Saracen hordes, the Virgin Mary wrapped herself in her blue kirtle and travelled over land and sea to Walsingham. She set up home in the Holy House beside the well.

A wooden statue of the Virgin was carved and set upon an altar in the Holy House. As the story of the miracle spread, the pilgrims came. They would kneel on a stone slab beside the well, ask for a blessing, throw a gift into the water and then enter the Holy House and come into the presence of Mary herself.

> Many sick have been cured by Our Lady's might,
> The dead restored to life, of this there is no doubt,
> The lame made whole, the blind restored to sight,
> Mariners vexed with tempest safe to port brought,
> The lover, the leper, the lunatic … all in this place
> Have been restored by Our Lady's Grace.

Lady Richeldis' son Geoffrey founded a priory there, and for 500 years Walsingham became one of England's most hallowed places of pilgrimage. It was visited by Henry III, Edward I, Edward II, Richard II, Henry VI, Henry VII, and Henry VIII who walked barefoot from East Barsham Manor.

In time the statue of the Virgin became festooned with gifts of gold and silver, and the Holy House glittered with precious stones. The priory and the townspeople of Walsingham prospered. Erasmus described a visit to the shrine:

> It is a small chapel made of wainscot, some twenty-four feet long by thirteen wide. Entrance is made by a narrow, little door. There is no light save only from wax candles. A most grateful fragrance meets the nostrils. It glitters on all sides with jewels, gold and silver. One canon attends the altar – a kind of pious shame brings some to the point that they give if anyone is watching, though they would not if no observer was present … as well as the statue of the Virgin there is also a finger of St Peter, the milk of the Holy Virgin encased in crystal, a piece of wood upon which the Virgin once rested and even the 'secret parts' of the Virgin in the shape of a toad-stone, for she alone hath over-come all earthly passions and trodden them underfoot.

Henry VIII's barefoot pilgrimage had been made to give thanks for the birth of his son, Prince Henry. Unfortunately, the infant died and Henry's devotions took a turn. In order to sire a son he wanted to divorce Catherine of Aragon and marry the Norfolk beauty Anne Boleyn. The Pope wouldn't grant him a divorce, so by the Act of Supremacy he made himself Supreme Ruler of the Church of England and divorced her himself. Then, in 1536, being short of money, he dissolved the monasteries, appropriating their incomes and assets. The Augustinian abbey at Walsingham had its money, treasures, plates and jewels sequestered; its stone, lands, and even the lead from its roof were sold.

There was outrage across England. A great body of protesters, 'The Pilgrimage of Grace', marched southwards to challenge the King's authority. In Walsingham the sub-prior Canon Nicholas

Mileham and the lay chorister Ralph Rogerson plotted a Norfolk insurrection that would join the Pilgrimage. But they were betrayed, and in the Martyr's Field at Walsingham, they were hanged, drawn and quartered as traitors.

In 1538 the carved image of the Virgin Mary, festooned with gold and silver, was taken to London. Archbishop Latimer pronounced: 'She hath been the devil's instrument and hath, I fear, brought many to eternal fire. Now she – with her sisters from Ipswich, Doncaster and Worcester – shall make a merry muster at Smithfield. I warrant they will not be all day in burning.'

And so it was that an ancient association between the Goddess and the well-spring, an association that probably pre-dated Lady Richeldis by many thousands of years, was brought abruptly to an end in Walsingham.

> As you came from the holy land
> Of Walsinghame
> Mett you not with my true love
> By the way you came?
>
> How shall I your trew love know
> That have mett many-a-one
> As I went to the holy land
> That have come, that have gone?
>
> She is neither white nor brown
> Butt as the heavens fair,
> There is none hath a form so divine
> In the earth or the air.
>
> Such a one did I meet, good sir,
> Such an angelyke face
> Who like a queen, like a nymph did appear
> By her gait, by her grace.

She hath left me here all alone
All alone as unknowne,
who once did me lead with her selfe
And loved me as her owne.

The Holy Rood of Bromholm

The ruins of the once well-endowed Cluniac priory at Bromholm are now part of a farm to the south of Bacton. It's difficult to imagine that it was once the proud possessor of one of the most sacred relics of the English church.

The True Cross was found by Saint Helena when she visited the Holy Land in the early fourth century. She divided it into nine parts, one for each of the nine orders of angels. The piece of wood that had been most sprinkled by the blood of Christ she fashioned into the shape of a cross. She kept it in a golden chest encrusted with precious stones. When she died, it passed to her son, the Emperor Constantine. Inevitably it ended up in Constantinople.

After the plundering of Constantinople in 1204, a flood of objects associated with the Passion poured into Europe. A cleric who claimed to have been chaplain to Baldwin of Constantinople fled to England with as many relics as he could lay his hands on. His name was Hugh. Among them was a wooden cross, as wide as a man's opened hand. Hugh's attempts to persuade the major English monasteries of the provenance of what seemed to be little more than a rough-hewn piece of wood met with no success. But the monks of Bromholm dug deep into their pockets and bought it from him.

They soon discovered that they had acquired the real thing. Thirty-nine corpses were restored to life by it. Huge numbers of blind, lame, leprous and possessed people were healed. Pilgrims flooded into Bromholm from all over Britain and Europe, and from an obscure foundation it achieved an undreamed-of prosperity.

The Paston family became patrons of Bromholm. In 1466 John Paston's funeral took place at the priory, so that he could be buried within the sphere of influence of the Holy Rood. His funeral feast involved the slaughtering of forty-one pigs, forty-nine calves and ten head of cattle. In total 1,300 eggs were consumed, and twenty gallons of milk, eight gallons of cream, thirteen barrels of beer, twenty-eight barrels of ale and a runlet of wine of fifteen gallons were quaffed. Twenty pounds of gold was struck into coins to be distributed among the poor.

By the time of the Dissolution of the Monasteries though, Bromholm's glory days were over, and the priory had only four monks, all of whom were accused of incontinence, and an income of only £100 per year.

The Holy Rood was taken to London and almost certainly burnt … although there is a tradition that it was rescued by the Pastons. Apparently it turned up in a convent in Yorkshire, where a Paston had once been a prioress. And then it appeared again during the Falklands War. One of the ships is said to have carried a piece of the True Cross, and when it was sunk, according to urban legend, the British Navy sent an underwater special forces team to make sure it was recovered.

7

THE PEDDLAR
OF SWAFFHAM

In the choir of Swaffham Church, the Victorian clergy stalls have incorporated some Medieval woodcarvings. On the south side there is the image of a man with a pack on his back, below him is a muzzled dog. On the north side there is the image of a man in a shop, with a woman looking out of a shop door below him. They used to be part of the family pew of John Chapman, a church warden and benefactor of the church who lived in the early 1400s. The carvings represent the beginning and end of his story.

John Chapman was a peddlar (or chapman) who travelled the highways and by-ways of Norfolk selling mirrors, scissors, thimbles, ribbons, relics and remedies. He was too poor to own a horse or donkey and carried his wares in a pack on his back. His only companion was a dog that was as quick after a rat or a rabbit as any dog in Norfolk.

John Chapman lived on the edge of Swaffham in a thatched hut of wattle and daub that was so patched and paltry that in winter the winds blew from room to room. In summer, the birds built their nests in the beams and rafters above his bed. He did have one little bit of good fortune though: behind the hut there was a garden, and in it an apple tree. Every autumn the tree would drop its fruit onto the grass – the sweetest apples in Swaffham.

One night, John Chapman was lying asleep under his thin blanket when he heard an angelic voice, as clear as moonlight: 'Go to London Bridge.'

He woke. The room was dark and the dog was snoring at the foot of the bed.

'It's nothing but a dream.'

He rolled over and went back to sleep. But the next night the voice returned.

'Go to London Bridge.'

Again John took no notice. But night after night the voice returned, and always the words were the same. John began to wonder: 'Maybe a man should listen to his dreams.' He rolled up his blanket and slung it over his shoulder. He filled a bag with bread and cheese and hung it from his belt. He whistled for his dog and set off for London Bridge.

He followed the Peddars Way, the straight lane that went southwards to Thetford. Then he took the old road that became the Icknield Way through Newmarket, Royston and Baldock. When he met the Great North Road, he journeyed into London. It was on the third day that he came, at last, to London Bridge. It stretched across the River Thames – the widest river he'd every clapped eyes upon – and had shops to either side of it. When he crossed the river he forgot he was on a bridge at all. It seemed, rather, to be a long, narrow street.

The bridge was a chaos of merchants, pilgrims, beggars, soldiers and drunkards. There was the shrieking of women selling cheese and honey. There was the neighing and stamping of horses, the shouting of bargemen. There was the smell of foul water and spices. John Chapman's senses were bombarded. He walked backwards and forwards over the bridge ... but nothing happened. The night came, shop doors were locked and bolted ... still nothing happened. John went down to the embankment under the bridge. He wrapped himself in his blanket and slept while his dog chased London rats.

The next morning he climbed back up to the bridge. All his food was gone, his belly was yawning and groaning with hunger ... and still nothing happened. He walked backwards and forwards to keep himself warm. Then he sat on a doorstep and shivered with cold: 'Why did I waste my time listening to dreams?'

It was as he was sitting there that a shopkeeper, a spice merchant, came out of his shop.

'Stranger, what are you doing here? All yesterday I watched you wandering to and fro across the bridge, and again this morning … and here you are, shivering like a lost soul. What's the matter with you?'

John Chapman turned: 'Well, I had a dream, and in it I heard a voice as clear as moonlight; it said 'Go to London Bridge' over and over, night after night … so I came.'

The shopkeeper threw back his head and laughed.

'Dreams! You don't want to take any notice of dreams, my friend. I'll tell you something. Last night I had a ridiculous dream. I dreamed I was in a place … what was it called … aha I remember, it was called Swaffham.'

John Chapman pricked up his ears.

'There was a little hut half open to the weather and behind it stood an apple tree … and there I was in my dream with a spade in my hands. I was digging among the roots of the tree. The blade of the spade struck a pot, and when I lifted it out of the ground it was filled with gold. But do you think I'm going to cross half of England in search of dream gold? Not me! Now you take my advice my friend, if I was you, I'd …'

But he looked, and John Chapman was gone. He was running through the streets of London with his dog at his heels. And he didn't stop running by day or by night until he came to Swaffham.

He fetched a spade and began to dig among the roots of the tree. Sure enough there was the scraping of the blade of the spade against something hard and curved. He loosened the soil, reached down and felt the rim of a pot. He heaved it out of the ground and tipped it onto its side. Yellow gold poured onto the grass. There were words scratched onto the side of the pot, but John could neither read nor write, so they meant nothing to him. But being of a devout nature, and fearing that this might be the Devil's work, he hid the treasure under the straw beneath his bed and took the pot to the parish priest who knew his ABCs.

The priest read the words aloud:

'Under me doth lie
another richer than I.'

John Chapman ran back to his hut, seized the spade and dug deeper. The priest followed him and stood at the wicker gate watching. This time the pot was too heavy for one man to lift alone. So the priest helped. They heaved it up and tipped it over. This treasure was twice the size of the first.

And so John Chapman's fortunes took a turn. He used the gold to pay for the building of a fine house in Swaffham Marketplace. He became a merchant and had his shop and store-houses there. He married a handsome Swaffham girl; she can be seen with her rosary in the carving in Swaffham church. He became a church-warden, with his own pew. And when he died in 1462, he left the greater part of his fortune for the rebuilding of Swaffham church.

As you enter it today your breath is taken away by the hammer-beam roof with its wooden angels, their wings outstretched … all thanks to John Chapman's bequest.

There's a carving of him in the market place too, on the village sign. But it's said that there was an older one once; long gone now, a statue of John Chapman with his dog at his heels, and carved into the stone at the foot of it were these words: 'Even dreams can turn to gold'.

8

SIR THOMAS ERPINGHAM

The main approach to Norwich Cathedral from Tombland is through the Erpingham Gate. It was built by Sir Thomas Erpingham shortly before his death in 1422. Sir Thomas himself can be seen kneeling in a niche in the centre of its flint-faced gable. He was a major player in the turbulent power struggles of Medieval England. He was knighted by John of Gaunt, fought in Spain, Scotland, Lithuania, Prussia and Jerusalem. He supported the cause of Gaunt's son Henry Bolingbroke; he was instrumental in overthrowing Richard II and installing Henry on the throne. And finally, as an old man, he commanded the archers at Agincourt for Gaunt's grandson Henry V. He is immortalised by Shakespeare: it is 'good old' Sir Thomas's cloak that King Harry borrows to go out disguised among his men on the morning of the battle of Agincourt.

Sir Thomas lived at Blickling Hall, and the Erpingham Hundreds had long been his family's estate. (It was another favourite of Shakespeare's, Sir John Fastolf, who bought Blickling from the Erpinghams in 1422).

But although he might have been 'good' and 'old' in Shakespeare's play, there is a legend that the Erpingham Gate was built as an act of penance for a much more scurrilous episode in Sir Thomas' life.

There was a Norwich friar called Brother John, who lusted after Sir Thomas' wife, Joan. During Mass, he pressed a letter into her hand. When she unfolded and read it, her pale face was suffused with blushes. Not only had Brother John expressed his passion for her; he had also suggested a time they might meet, a trysting place, and had given some intimation of his sexual prowess. Joan, being a faithful and devoted wife, showed the letter to her husband. Sir Thomas smiled grimly: 'We shall soon satisfy ourselves of this saintly stallion.'

He went to Joan's 'garderobe' and selected a dress. At the prescribed time he and a faithful servant rode to the trysting place, beneath a willow on the river bank not far from the friary. The servant waited with his horse some distance away. Sir Thomas dressed himself in women's clothes, with a silken scarf over his head. It was dusk as he leaned against the trunk of the tree, looking out towards the water, and waited. Soon he heard footsteps; then he felt plump warm hands on his hips, then breath against his neck: 'You have come, my sweetheart.'

Sir Thomas turned. The friar saw the grizzled face of a veteran of many bloody campaigns. He turned to run. Sir Thomas reached beneath his skirts, pulled out an iron hammer, and brought it down onto the friar's bald, shining pate.

Friar John dropped to his knees. He fell flat on his face, shuddered and lay still. Sir Thomas turned him over. He knelt beside him. There was no breath, no pulse. There could be no doubting it; the friar was dead.

'By Our Lady, I've killed him!'

The servant came forward from his hiding place. Sir Thomas turned to him: 'I had intended to give him a drubbing he would never forget, but now the damned lecher is dead … what shall we do with him?'

The servant was not lost for an answer.

'He only has a small dent in his head, my lord; let's carry him to the Friary and prop him against a wall.'

They slung the friar across a horse, carried him to the friary grounds, lifted him over a wall and arranged him in a sitting position on the far side.

The corpse hadn't been there for long when another friar, Brother Richard, caught sight of Brother John, fast asleep when he should have been at prayer. Brother Richard was a pious man, but the sight of that notorious womaniser dozing against a wall in the moonlight was too much for him. He picked up a stone and threw it at him. The stone struck the side of Brother John's head and he slumped onto the ground. Brother Richard ran forward. He was dead, with a dent in his head.

'I have killed him, I have sinned against God and man and killed poor Brother John.'

Brother Richard lifted the corpse onto the top of the wall, and rolled it over so that it fell down on the far side. Then he fetched a pony and rode away from the scene of his crime.

A little while later, Sir Thomas' faithful servant was riding past the friary when he saw the corpse again, lying on the wrong side of the wall.

'Well, well, we meet again my friend. And this time I'll get rid of you for good and all!'

He climbed down from the horse's back and lifted the corpse into the saddle. He fitted his feet into the stirrups. The body, now stiff with rigor mortis, sat bolt upright. He tied the reins around the corpse's wrists.

'Away with you!' He slapped the horse's rump and it set off at a gallop.

Brother Richard, riding out of Norwich, heard the sound of hooves pounding behind him. He looked over his shoulder and saw Brother John, pale in the moonlight, galloping towards him. The dead monk came up alongside him, toppled and fell onto the ground at his feet.

Brother Richard dismounted, trembling with terror. This was clearly a divine intervention; his guilt had caught up with him and he must confess.

The next day he went to the bishop, Henry de Spencer, and told all. He was sentenced to death. But as he stood beneath the gallows with the hood over his head and the noose swinging at the ready, Sir Thomas Erpingham came galloping through the crowd.

'Hangman, hold your hand!'

Sir Thomas, the most powerful knight in Norfolk, lifted Friar Richard down from the scaffold. Then he knelt before Bishop de Spencer and confessed that in truth the blood of Friar John was on his hands and his hands only. He told his story. And when he had finished, given the circumstances of the death, he was forgiven … but as a penance for manslaughter, he agreed to pay for the building of the Erpingham Gate.

Well, that's one version of the story. The other tells of how Henry de Spencer, Bishop of Norwich, had been a supporter of Richard II. When Richard was deposed and (probably) murdered at Pontefract, de Spencer was disgraced. Sir Thomas Erpingham had been in exile with Henry Bolingbroke, had helped him secure the throne, had captured Richard and had (almost certainly) advised that he be done away with. As a result, a terrible rift opened between Erpingham and the divines of Norwich Cathedral. It was to heal this wound and to ensure that his bones would be laid to rest in the cathedral, that as an old man, Sir Thomas built his gate.

The lavish tomb of Sir Thomas and his two wives is gone from the chancel of the cathedral (the kneeling figure in the gate might once have been a part of it) … but his reputation remains as one of Norfolk's most distinguished sons; a shrewd and loyal player on the world stage.

And written over and again into his gate is one word, his last piece of advice to the generations that have followed him: 'yenk', meaning 'think'.

9

WITCHES

In October 2011, while the Duke's Head Hotel in the Tuesday Marketplace in Kings Lynn was being renovated, the bones of a cat were found in the ceiling of room ten. They were almost certainly put there to ward off the spirits of witches – and with good reason. The Tuesday Marketplace has witnessed the grisly deaths of several unfortunate women … and one of them is supposed to haunt the hotel. It is the ghost of a servant girl, boiled alive in 1531 for stealing a purse of money from her master.

In 1590 Margaret Read was burned alive as a witch there. It is said that at the moment of her death, her heart burst from her body and struck the brickwork of a building on the north side of the market place. The spot is still marked by a small diamond that has been cut into the brickwork and encloses a heart, about 12ft from the ground.

But the witch we know the most about is Mary Smith, hanged in Kings Lynn on 19 January 1616. A full account of her alleged spells and curses is included in A. Roberts' *A treatise of Witchcraft*. And we have to take the word of a credulous Jacobean divine for all that follows.

Mary Smith was married to Henry Smith, a Kings Lynn glover. She was a cheese-seller. Several of her neighbours were engaged in the same trade and when she saw them get a higher price for their cheeses than she had managed, she flew into a passion, cursed them and 'became incensed with unruly passions'. The Devil, ' who is skilful and rejoiceth at such an occasion offered, and knoweth how to stir up the evil affected humours of corrupt minds', appeared before her dressed in black. He spoke to her in a 'low, hissing voice', telling her that if she continued in her malice, envy and hatred, then he would be 'revenged for her upon all those to whom she willed evil'. And so Mary entered a compact with the Devil, renouncing God and 'betaking herself to him'.

This was not the only time the Devil appeared to Mary Smith. He came to her regularly, so that he could hold her in his possession, sometimes as an enclosing mist, sometimes as a 'ball of fire with some dispersed spangles of black'. The last time she saw him, she was in prison and about to be brought to trial. He was as she had seen him the first time, but now his horns were clearly visible. He told her to confess nothing and to stay true, but this time she refused him.

Having made her initial compact, the first to suffer from Mary's new-found power and 'taste the gall of her bitterness' was her neighbour John Orkton. He was a sailor who had recently returned from the Netherlands. For some reason Mary's son annoyed him and he gave him a wallop. The boy cried out, and Mary came to the door of her house. When she saw her son in tears she turned to the sailor: 'I wish the fingers on your hand would rot off!'

He shrugged and went home. But soon he grew weak and 'distempered in stomach', he could digest no food, and the sickness spread to his hands and feet so that his fingers corrupted and were cut off. His toes also putrefied 'in a very strange and admirable manner.'

Despite this, he still went to sea, but never again made a prosperous voyage either to himself or to the owners of the ship. He consulted a doctor in Yarmouth but no medicine had any effect. Finally he came home and took to his bed. And Mary, rejoicing at the calamity, was rumoured to have said: 'Orkton now lyeth a-rotting.'

And though, it was admitted, she had shown some kindness to her neighbour in his affliction, it had only been 'to plaster over and disguise her former barbarous action'.

The next to suffer at her hands was Elizabeth Hancocke, a young widow. Mary accused her of stealing her hen, saying, 'I wish her bones would stick in your throat'. Elizabeth took little notice, but when she came to her house, she saw the hen sitting above the door. She seized it, brought it back to Mary and ticked her off for casting untrue aspersions on honest neighbours. At this Mary flew into a rage: 'You proud Jinny, you proud flirt … may the pox light upon you!'

That night Elizabeth sickened and was 'pinched at the heart', became weak and lost all appetite. Over the following days, whenever Mary saw her, standing pale and sick in her doorway taking the air, she shouted: 'The pox light upon you, can you yet come to the door?'

The sickness got worse, and she became 'so grievously racked and tormented through all parts of her body, as if the very flesh had been torn from the bones.'

At last Elizabeth's father Edward Drake went to visit a 'cunning man' (male witch), to see if he could get the better of Mary.

'Tis well you came, for one day longer and her heart would have been spent … and all on account of a hen.'

It was the first Edward Drake had heard of the hen, but it would later be verified as true.

'There is a remedy, but you must keep silence on the matter, for the woman who has done this to Elizabeth will know anything. Here she is!'

He held up a dark glass and in it Drake saw the image of Mary Smith's face.

'Now listen to me and do what I tell you …'

He whispered into Edward Drake's ear, and gave him a bottle of black ointment like treacle, a twist of powder, and some words written on paper.

He did as he had been told. He bought flour and mixed it with his daughter's urine. He made it into a cake and baked it on the hearth. He spread the ointment and sprinkled the powder over it. He stuck the words to it. Then he cut the cake in two. Half to go on Elizabeth's breast over her heart, half to go under. All this time, he had kept silent. And soon the magic had its effect. His daughter began to regain her strength. Two days later, father and daughter were strolling along the street when Mary Smith saw them: 'Aha, so ye've been to a wizard and have made a witch-cake … I'll learn soon enough how you came to have such knowledge!'

Mary had a familiar, a cat, which began to frequent Elizabeth's house. Elizabeth's lover tried to chase it away; he ran it through with a sword, he struck it with a pike-staff – but the cat would take no injury … and soon enough Elizabeth was sick again.

The third to suffer was Cecily Balye. She was a servant, and one morning, as she was sweeping the street before her master's door, Mary Smith picked a quarrel with her about the manner of her sweeping. The quarrel got more and more heated until Mary shouted: 'You are a great fat-tailed sow – but that fatness shall shortly be pulled down and abated.'

The next night Mary Smith's cat entered Cecily's bedchamber and sat upon her breast, so that she could hardly draw breath. She opened her eyes and saw Mary herself in the chamber where she lay. Mary whispered: 'As long as you live near me you shall not be well, but grow from evil to worse.'

From that moment, Cecily began to languish and 'grew exceeding lean', and it was only when she moved to another household that she recovered.

Cecily also glimpsed Mary through 'a cranny whereof she looked' making an adoration to the Devil 'in submissive manner, upon her knees, with strange gestures, uttering many murmuring, broken and imperfect speeches'.

The fourth and final victim was Edmund Holland, a shoemaker and cheese merchant. He had threatened her business by purchasing several 'bargains of Holland cheese' and reselling them at a knock-down price. From that day onwards, whenever Edmund bought a cheese he was afflicted with a terrible pain in his leg. Then, one night, a spirit in Mary's likeness appeared in his bedchamber and whisked about his face a wet cloth 'of very loathsome savour'. He covered his face with his hands and when he looked again he saw at the foot of the bed a little man 'clothed in russet with a little bush beard'. He told Edmund he had come to heal his leg, but when Edmund saw he had cloven hooves he refused the offer and the demon vanished out of sight. At this point in his account, the author sees fit to interject, 'These being no vain conceits or fantasies, but well advised and diligently considered observances.'

Edmund was, from that point onwards, possessed by a madness or frenzy so that he was 'distracted and deprived of all sense', although with periods of release so that 'for thirteen or fourteen weeks together he would be of perfect memory'.

Mary sent another of her imps in the shape of a toad to Edmund's house. One of Edmund's apprentices seized it and threw it into the fire. At that moment Mary Smith endured torturing pains, 'testifying the felt grief by her outcrys then made'.

It was common knowledge that a witch's hold could be broken if her blood was drawn, so Edmund tried to scratch Mary … but his nails 'turned like feathers and had no strength to harm her'.

On the strength of these testimonies from her neighbours, the fierce-tongued Mary Smith was brought to trial. History does not relate the form the trial took, whether she was 'ducked or swum' in the River Ouse, whether she was 'pricked' to discover the places the Devil had left his mark, whether she was 'starved' and deprived of sleep (all common practices). Eventually she confessed her guilt, and on 19 January was brought to the scaffold. A huge crowd had gathered in the Tuesday Marketplace (and no doubt there were watchers through the windows of the Duke's Head Hotel). Mary was asked if she would be contented to have a psalm sung. She answered that she would and asked that it be 'The Lamentation of a Sinner', whose first line is 'Lord, turn not thy face away'.

When the psalm was finished Mary Smith was hanged. A. Roberts finishes his account with these words: 'In the judgement of charity we are to conceive the best, and think she resteth in peace, notwithstanding her heinous transgressions formerly committed: for there is no malady incurable to the Almighty Physician.'

10

Four Ballad Tales

The Babes in the Wood

When, in August 1879, a lightning bolt struck down a mighty oak tree in Wayland Wood (at 5ft from the ground it had a circumference of 12ft), people came from all over Norfolk for souvenirs. It was the oak tree that had witnessed the most poignant moment of a story that – in ballad form – was known across the English-speaking world.

There was once a Norfolk nobleman and his wife who were struck down by the plague. Knowing that they were not long for this world they called their closest relative, the woman's brother, to their bedside. With such strength as was left to him, the nobleman whispered his last request: 'Look after our children; they shall have no friend in the world but you when we are gone. When young Tom comes of age, he shall inherit £300 a year. And little Kate, when she gets wed, shall have as dowry £500 in gold.'

And then his wife uttered her last words: 'Dear brother, treat them kindly, and, god-willing, they shall grow up strong and happy ... but if, by chance, they perish and join us in paradise, then it is written into our will that their money will pass to you.'

The little ones – aged three and two – came to the bedside and their parents kissed them with lips as cold as stone.

Their brother dropped to his knees, seized the trembling hands of his sister and brother-in-law, and in a voice choked with sobs swore a solemn oath:

> God never prosper me nor mine
> Nor aught else that I have
> If I do wrong your children dear
> When you're laid in your grave.

And so the nobleman and his wife died with their hearts at ease. But no sooner were they safely laid in the family vault, than the nobleman hired a couple of cut-throats (in one version of the story their names are given as Rawbones and Wouldkill).

'Take these two tiresome little brats into Wayland Wood and slit their throats; bury them so that even the foxes won't find them'. He pulled two purses from his pocket. 'And you can have £50 a-piece for your trouble.'

The two men took the money, sharpened their knives, and set off into the wood (just to the south of Watton, and much bigger then than it is now). Each held a child by the hand. But the children skipped and prattled; they tugged at the cut-throats' arms to pick things up; they sang snatches of songs and took such a delight in the bright, dappled day, that the two men began to have second thoughts. When they reached the thicket that was to have been the scene of the ghastly crime, one turned to the other: 'I've cut a good score of throats before today, but these two tender necks I shall not scratch.'

The other shook his head: 'They're a pretty little pair I grant you … but £50 is £50, and we've our reputations to consider.'

'Well, I shall not harm them.'

'Then I'll do the job single-handed.'

He pulled his knife from its sheath.

'Oh no you won't.'

The tender-hearted cut-throat (let's call him Rawbones) drew his knife and fell upon his companion. A terrible fight followed; the brown bracken and the green grass was splattered with red blood, and soon enough Wouldkill lay dead with a wound to the heart. Rawbones drew out his knife, wiped it clean on a mossy bank, and called to the children. 'Now then my little ones, you need not fear me. I'll do you no harm.'

He reached into Wouldkill's jacket, fished out a purse, and dropped it into his own pocket.

'I'll not scratch you, my little friends.'

He kissed the little boy and girl on the forehead with his bristly lips.

'Now you mind how I done you kindly … and if I can, I'll come back for you with bread and cake.'

He ducked out of sight and disappeared into the shadows of the wood.

The two children, hand in hand, wandered this way and that way. They ate blackberries, but they weren't enough to slake their thirst or fill their empty bellies. Soon they were crying with hunger. When the night came, they huddled together and slept in each other's arms. In the morning they wandered and crawled, and at last, weak from lack of food, they lay down in the shade of a huge oak tree and tucked themselves among the dead leaves between two twisting roots. It was there that they breathed their last.

It's at this moment in the ballad that the verse appeared that ensured its place in every Victorian parlour-room repertoire:

No burial this pretty pair
From any man receives,
But Robin Redbreast piously
Did cover them with leaves.

And so the children were discovered, covered with leaves, under the oak in Wayland Wood. Their uncle, feigning sorrow, buried them and claimed their inheritance. But from the moment of the children's death, his oath at his sister's deathbed began to catch up with him. His barns caught fire, his cattle wasted, and his own two sons drowned on a trip to Portugal. Within seven years his lands were pawned and mortgaged and he was dead in a debtor's prison.

And as for Rawbones, it's said that he was arrested for robbery; he was brought to trial and was condemned to death. On the scaffold he made a confession and told the whole story of the babes in the wood. He told of how he had returned to Wayland Wood with bread and cake, but the children had wandered from the thicket where he'd left them. He'd searched and not been able to find them.

'May God take their tender souls to His bosom ... who shall not spare mine.'

And with those words the hatch opened, the rope tightened and his life ended.

And it's said that from that day to this, the crying of the two children can still be heard, and it is for that reason that the wood is known as 'Wailing Wood' as well as 'Wayland Wood'.

The story of 'The Babes in the Wood' has a historical precedent. In Griston Old Hall (just to the east of Wayland Wood), lived the de Grey family. The heir to the estate, Thomas, was married as a seven year old boy to Elizabeth Drury, aged six. When his father died Thomas was taken into the care of his uncle Robert de Grey until he came of age. But Thomas was killed under mysterious circumstances and his uncle set about claiming the de Grey property from Thomas's child-widow. Robert de Grey, like the uncle in the story, died in 1601 with debts totalling £1,780.

That's as maybe, but certainly by the Victorian era the story had become so firmly associated with Wayland Wood that when the great oak was shattered by lightning, crowds gathered to take home relics of the pitiful tale.

Another parallel story is told in Bradwell. In the north wall of the church, beside the altar, is the painted monument of William Vesey, who died in 1644. He is shown with his two wives and two surviving sons. In relief, below them, are depicted his four daughters, two to either side of a recumbent little boy with a skull. Local tradition says the monument shows how the four girls found the body of their little brother, who had got lost and perished in Bradwell Wood.

THE GREAT OAK

Sir Thomas Kuyvet of Ashwellthorpe Hall (south-east of Wymondham) was knighted by Elizabeth I during her state journey through Norfolk in 1578. He was famous as a generous host, and his banquets were legendary. A curious incident took place during one of them that became the subject of a ballad.

Sir Thomas' guests were gathering at the hall, anticipating the usual good cheer, when one of them, a stranger from London, stepped forward. He raised his voice above the general chatter: 'Before we dine, I should like to show you a wonder.'

The crowd fell silent. He reached into his pocket and pulled out an acorn. It was passed around the banqueting hall from hand to hand.

'Now watch.'

There was a crack between the floor-boards. He dropped the acorn into it. Straight away there came the sound of splintering, and before the eyes of the assembled company an oak sapling burst out of the floor. It spread its branches across the ceiling, its trunk thickened; its twigs budded and leaved. Then acorns swelled and dropped like hail stones onto the heads of Sir Thomas and his guests.

Sir Thomas clapped his hands and laughed, and ordered his swineherds to drive his pigs into the hall. They feasted happily on the acorns. When they had gobbled every last one, Sir Thomas turned to the Londoner:

'How can we bring in the boards for supper with this tree filling the hall?'

The stranger shrugged.

'It must be cut down.'

Sir Thomas called his foresters and they set to work with their axes.

I'll tell you here no lye
The chips then there did fly
Buzzing about like flies
That men were forced to ward,
Their faces well to guard
For fear they'd lose their eyes.

Before long, the tree was felled and its trunk lay across the floor of the hall.

The stranger smiled at Sir Thomas: 'Now it must be lifted and carried out.'

All the guests came forward to help:

He bid them then be bold
And every one take hold
This oak for to carry away,
And all they hold did get
But e'd not stirr a whit
But still along it lay.

For all their panting and heaving, the tree wouldn't budge. The stranger watched and laughed. Then he lifted his fingers to his mouth and whistled. In through the door, one behind the other, came a pair of little yellow, downy goslings. They tucked their beaks under the oak, lifted it and carried it out of the hall. The company ran outside to see what had become of the tree … but there was no trace of it to be seen … and inside every chip, acorn, leaf and broken twig was gone … as though the whole strange episode had been a vision or a dream.

The stranger bowed, and Sir Thomas, delighted, called for the boards to be set in place and laden with 'capon, ham, beef, venison, mutton and a hogshead of Rhenish that we may drink the health of our cunning Londoner'.

The ballad ends:

> This story is true
> Which I have told you.

THE YARMOUTH TRAGEDY

Whether there is any historical precedent for this ballad story, I do not know. It has a wide currency and is more common now in the blue-grass repertoire of the USA than in English folk clubs.

The ballad tells of beautiful Nancy of Yarmouth, a merchant's daughter (I imagine them living in a fine house on the South Quay), heiress to £1,500 a year. She fell in love with Jem, a local boy of modest means, and they resolved to marry. When Nancy's parents got wind of the romance, they tried to put a stop to it – arguing that with her charms and fortune, she would be a fitting wife for a lord of the realm. But Nancy shook her head:

> Jemmy's the man that I admire,
> He is the riches that I adore.
> To be a great one I never desire
> My heart is fixed to have no more.

No word from her parents could dissuade her from her purpose. Finally, Nancy's father summoned Jem to the parlour of his house. Through the window he could see his fleet of ships moored at the quayside. He looked the youth up and down.

'Very well, you shall have her, but on one condition.'

'What is that, Sir?'

'That you show me you are man enough to be worthy of her. I want you to go as a sailor on my ship the *Mary Galley* to Barbados. When you return, Nancy will be yours.'

Secretly he was hoping that a storm, or the scurvy, or the lure of sweet living on Barbados would ensure that he never came home.

Nancy was called into the room and the condition of marriage was explained to her. She threw herself into Jem's arms and thrust a ring onto his finger.

'Bear it with you wherever you go … no one alive shall enjoy me but you.'

As soon as the ship had set sail, the merchant and his wife invited lords of birth and breeding to court Nancy – but she slighted all their favours.

Meanwhile, Jem had arrived at Barbados. Being 'handsome in each feature' a Barbadan woman quickly fixed her eyes on him. She dressed herself in rich attire, plaited her hair with precious stones and approached him, attended by a hundred slaves.

> In robes of gold I will deck thee
> Pearls and rich jewels I'll lay at thy feet
> In a chariot of gold you'll ride with pleasure
> If you can love me – answer me straight.

Jem, 'amaz'd with wonder,' shook his head: 'Forbear, Madam, in Old England I'm pledged to a lady – she has my heart, and I only have one to give.'

At these words the woman 'raved in distraction':

> A curious jewel then she gave him,
> Within her hand she held a knife;
> One fatal stroke ere he could stop her,
> Did put an end to her tender life.

There was great lamentation for the dead woman on Barbados … but Jem had been tested and had been proved true. Soon enough, the *Mary Galley* was sailing home to Yarmouth.

But word of this story, and of Jem's return, reached Nancy's father. He saw that desperate means were required.

> When her father found that he was coming
> A letter he writ to the Boatswain, his friend,
> Saying a handsome reward I will give you
> If you the sweet life of young Jemmy will end.

And so it was that, one evening, as Jem was leaning over the rails of the quarter deck staring into the churning waves, he was seized from behind and thrown into the water. His cries went unheard and he was drowned in the dark waters of the Atlantic Ocean.

That night, Nancy was lying in her bedchamber when she heard a voice calling her name from the street below. She drew the curtains, opened the casement and looked down. There was Jem. He was looking up and waving to her.

> Her nightgown embroidered with silver and gold
> Carelessly around her body she throws
> With her two maids at hand to attend her
> To meet her true lover she instantly goes.

She ran down the stairs and out into the street. She threw her arms around his neck and kissed him. Then she drew away.

'My love, your lips are colder than clay.'

He looked at her, paler than death in the flickering oil lamp of the quayside.

> I for your sake refused gold and silver
> Riches and jewels did I despise.
> A charming lady did for me expire
> Thinking of thee I was deaf to her cries.
>
> Your cruel parents have been my undoing
> And now I sleep in a watery tomb …

And so, for your promise dear, I am suing
Dead or alive you are my own.

'Dearest one, I am yours and yours only.'

She seized his hand and drew him to the water's brink. The two maids, who could not see the ghost, followed behind, thinking that she was in some strange state of distraction. They saw her stand a moment on the quayside, then, before they could hold her back, she had leapt into the saltwater and vanished from sight.

Two or three days later the Boatswain looked down from the deck of the *Mary Galley* and saw the two lovers, entwined, rolling over and over in one another's arms in the swell of the sea as though they were in an ecstasy of love – though their eyes were empty and crawling with sea-worms.

Consumed with remorse for his crime he confessed the whole story.

On board ship he was tried for murder,
At the yard-arm he was hanged for the same,
Her father broke his heart for Nancy
Before the ship to harbour came.

And so the sorry story ends, but being a ballad, not without a moral:

Thus cursed gold caused distraction,
Why should the rich so covet gain?
I pray this tale may be a warning
That cruel parents don't do the same.

The Mistletoe Bough

Another ballad story that is still sung across England and North America is supposed to have had its origin in Brockdish Hall near Diss.

It tells of a midwinter wedding. After the family and guests had returned from church, after they had feasted and danced, the bride, being in high spirits, demanded of her new husband a game of hide and seek.

She seized a mistletoe bough (hoping to claim a kiss when she was found), ran up the wide wooden stairs and disappeared into darkness. The bridegroom waited, then lit a lantern and set off to seek his sweetheart. At first he searched light-heartedly, then in earnest, then calling her name … but there was no sign of her. After an hour he called on the company to help him.

They sought her that night and they sought her next day,
And they sought her in vain while a week passed away.

She had vanished without trace. Months and years passed, and the tragedy became a sorrowful tale. The broken-hearted bridegroom grew old.

And as he passed the children cried:
The old man weeps for his hidden bride.

And then, a hundred or so years later, a lumber-room in the attic
of Brockdish Hall was cleared. In a corner beside a brick chimney
there was a dust-covered chest. It was held shut by a sprung brass
clasp. When the lid was lifted a skeleton was found inside, dressed
in the mouldering remnants of a wedding dress, and clutching
between its finger-bones the dry twig of a mistletoe bough.

Oh sad was her fate – in sportive jest
She hid from her lord in the old oak chest.
It closed with a spring – and dreadful doom,
The bride lay clasped in a living tomb.
Oh the mistletoe bough
Oh the mistletoe bough.

11

Bells

The Norfolk coastline is one of the most mobile in Britain. Nine thousand years ago there was unbroken land between Norfolk and Denmark; an extensive lowland landscape with hills, rivers and lakes, sometimes called 'Doggerland'. With the rise of sealevels as the last of the glaciers melted, the land was inundated, so that by the Neolithic period the coastline was approximately the shape it is today. But the sea has never stopped its incursion. Since Roman times, 1½ miles of shoreline has disappeared from the North Norfolk coast. Shifting sandbeds and global warming are accelerating the process today. Happisburgh is disappearing before our eyes ... and as King Canute made clear to us more than 1000 years ago, nothing in our arsenal of human ingenuity can hold back the tide.

With the loss of land often comes a folk memory of kingdoms under the sea. But although a *Daily Mail* article about the excavation of Doggerland recently carried the headline: 'Britain's Atlantis found beneath the North Sea', Norfolk folklore doesn't have a Lyonesse, or an Ys or an Cantre'r Gwadod. What it does carry is something more humble and more poignant: the memory of sunken villages.

From the seafront at Cromer, if you look 200 yards beyond the end of the pier, you can see only water where the thriving port of Shipden once stood. Similarly, from Sea Palling the watery grave of Eccles can be viewed. Beyond Mundesley lies Clare, beyond Bacton lies Keswick, beyond Horsey lies Waxham Parva, beyond Happisburgh lies Wimpwell.

Lillian Rider-Haggard remembered Eccles church tower, before it was shattered by a tremendous storm in 1895, standing on the beach, the last remnant of the lost village:

> One September day years ago, when the tower of Eccles Church still stood on the dunes, there came a north-easterly gale and a 'scour' which swept the sand from the old graveyard, leaving the long outlines of the graves washed clean by the sea. In one lay an almost perfect skeleton embedded in the clay, the hollow-eyed skull gazing up at the limitless sweep of the sky.

If there is one sound that binds a community, it is the sound of its bells. Bells are rung for weddings and funerals, for matins, evensong and all the services of the church; for the hours of the day, to sound alarms for invasion and celebrations for victory. In the Medieval church the bells were named and blessed, 'christened', before they were hung.

It's not surprising then, that the lost communities of the sunken villages, their thresholds, hearths and bones washed by saltwater, are remembered by their bells. All along the Norfolk coast, there are stories of the bells in their sunken towers ringing out when the sea becomes choppy. It's as though the fishermen, salt-panners, spinners, weavers, merchants, farm-wives, cocklers, monks and shopkeepers of Shipden, Eccles, Clare and Waxham Parva are calling out not to be forgotten with the tongues of bells.

Whenever there's a storm, it's said, the bells can be clearly heard, ringing out beneath the waves.

And sometimes the lost towers make their presence felt in a more tangible story. In August 1888 a steamer tug called *Victoria* was carrying holidaymakers from Cromer to Yarmouth. When her engines had been started and she was several hundred yards out to sea there was a sudden grinding, searing sound, the ship's hull was torn open, and water began to pour into the hold. Local fishermen saw what had happened and came out with their boats to evacuate the passengers. Nobody was drowned.

On examination, the ship was reckoned to have struck the steeple of St Peter's church, Shipden. Accounts of what followed seem to varies, some say the tower was dynamited as a potential hazard, others that when the tide is exceptionally low the steeple can still be seen jutting above the waves. Either way, its ghostly bells are still heard booming out above the roar of wind and waves … and the best place to hear them is from the end of Cromer Pier.

Further inland, at Tunstall near Great Yarmouth, you can see the hollow belfry of the ruined church of St Peter & St Paul – only its chancel is still in use. It was destroyed by a terrible fire nearly 200 years ago. When the fire had exhausted itself and the church was a smouldering ruin, the parson decided to take the bells, which had crashed through the floor of the belfry, and sell them. 'The weight of bell-metal,' he thought, 'will fetch a pretty price'. He hired a cart and a company of ten men with ropes and levers to lift the bells from the ruin. He waited until nightfall, not wanting to attract undue attention to his labours, and set out for the church.

During the day his churchwardens had visited the ruin. They had looked at the bells lying in their bed of ashes, the metal still so hot that when they spat on it the spittle hissed and danced.

'That's more than a ton of bell-metal, I'll wager. If we could get it to the Whitechapel foundry, they'd pay us handsome money.'

They too borrowed a cart, hired several strong local lads to help them, and waited until nightfall for the bells to cool down.

There was a strong moon – a bull's moon – and the sleeping village was sharply lit in shades of black and grey and silver. As the parson with his cart and men drew close to the lych-gate, he heard the clopping of hooves and trundling of wheels behind him. He turned and saw another cart was approaching the church tower.

'What the devil are you after?'

The parson's men rolled up their sleeves, clenched their fists and squared up behind him.

'Same as what you are, I reckon.'

The churchwardens and their lads came forward.

The parson cocked his head.

'And what do you surmise that might be?'

One of the churchwardens winked at the others.

'If a bell can be christened, I reckon that can be buried ... and we've come to take these ones here to meet their maker!'

'Well, as parson, that's my privilege ... I'd move along homeward, unless you want a damn good drubbing.'

One of the churchwardens came forward and cuffed the parson on the ear.

'We ain't going nowhere, your reverence!'

And at that the rival armies fell upon each other, the parson in the thick of the fray, punching and grunting and wiping the blood from his lip.

Then, out of nowhere, there came a deafening clap of thunder. The fighters stopped and turned towards the tower. They saw the figure of a man towering above the ruined church. He was coal-black with eyes as red as the fires of hell. He had horns and hooves. He reached into the shattered tower and, one by one, picked up the six bells. He dropped them into a bag, turned and strode across the parish, stepping over walls and hedges as though they were no higher than kerbstones.

The parson, churchwardens and hired men followed the Devil, all animosity forgotten, the parson shouting words from the Holy Scriptures at the huge black back. When the infernal figure came to a group of elder trees, still known as Hell Carr, he threw back his head and bellowed. Beside the trees was a pit. He leapt into it, taking the bells with him.

When the men reached the edge of the pit, all they could see were bubbles rising to the surface.

And even to this day, if a visitor can find Hell Hole, beside Hall Carr, he or she can still see bubbles rising to the surface from the bells that are still sinking deeper and deeper into that bottomless pit.

Other Norfolk traditions link the taking of bells from their belfries with less self-interested motives. Perhaps there's some truth in the story that the gold and silver bells of Thetford Priory were buried, in secret, deep in the motte of Castle Hill. It's said that they were buried by monks during the reign of Henry VIII to save them from being confiscated by the King's agents at the time of the Dissolution of the Monasteries. Similarly in Attlebridge, there's a tradition that a set of silver bells were dropped into the mud and weed of the River Wensum to keep them from the gaze of Cromwell's men. Neither story tells whether or not the bells are there still.

And then, most lovely of all, is the tradition that in East Dereham, on Christmas morning, the bells of St Nicholas sing out of their own accord for pure joy that *Christus natus est*, 'Christ is born'.

12

STONE HEARTS

If brothers or sisters quarrel in the villages of Freethorpe, Halvergate or Wickhampton, there is a remedy readily available that has been used by generations of exasperated parents to put a quietness on their offspring. When the bickering has gone on for too long, a parent only has to say: 'You come along with me.'

He or she then grabs the children by the arms and frog-marches them to St Andrew's church in Wickhampton. Against the north wall lie two effigies; one of them clasps a stone heart in his hands.

'Do you know who these are?'

The children scuff at the stone floor with their shoes and shake their heads, still eyeing daggers at each other.

'Well, I'll tell you. These are two brothers; the Hampton brothers. One was lord of the manor here, and the other was lord of the manor in Halvergate. Could they get along? No they could not. They'd quarrelled from the cradle. And when they came to their inheritance each thought the other had done better. Each thought the other had been his daddy's favourite. Whenever they met, their eyes would smoulder with anger, and the few words they exchanged would be sharp as knives.

'Now at that time, and I'm going back 800 years or so, on the boundary where the two parishes met, there stood a very handsome tree, a sweet chestnut. It's long gone now, but in its day it dropped such an abundance of sweet, fat nuts that people would come from miles around to gather them.

'Well each of these brothers took the notion into his head that the tree belonged to him, and that any man or woman who was not of his parish had no right to a single nut from it. And each of them, with a band of armed retainers, decided to guard it against all trespassers.

'It would have been at first light on an October morning, with the nuts all prickled and ready to drop, that one brother strode northwards towards the boundary, little expecting that his hated brother was, at that very moment, striding southwards with the same intention.

'When the brothers saw each other, the anger that had been simmering since boyhood suddenly came to the boil. They drew their knives and fell upon each other with such savagery that their armed retainers could only stand and stare in astonishment. They shouted, they cursed, they stabbed, they gouged, they sliced and parried, they cut and tore. Then, with a shout of triumph and agony, each of the brothers staggered backwards and fell dead onto the ground.

'The retainers came forward to see what had happened. Each of the dead men was lying on the blood-soaked ground clutching a heart in his hand. Each of the Hampton brothers had, at the same moment, torn the living heart from his brother's body.

'Then there came a clap of thunder and a sudden, blinding flash of lightning. The retainers covered their faces with their hands.

When they opened their fingers and lowered their hands, they saw that the two brothers had been turned to stone. They looked at one another in awe: "Almighty God has wrought a miracle. We should take the stone bodies to the church and set them there as a warning to all brothers and sisters who see fit to quarrel and argue over nix-nought-nothing."

'They lifted the stone brothers onto their shoulders and carried them here to St Andrew's church. They set them where you see them now, each with the other's heart in his hands. And it's said that after the death of those two brothers the two parishes were given their names. One was called Wicked Hampton and the other Hellfire Gate. In time the names were whittled down to Wickhampton and Halvergate. One brother has been worn away over the years and the heart is gone. But look, the other's still holding his clear enough … Now, how about you two set your differences aside and head off home like Christians?'

Nine times out of ten the story works its magic and the children go home as meek as lambs. On the few occasions that the brothers or sisters are still at loggerheads, a parent has another trump card up his or her sleeve.

'Now you look up there.'

On the church wall is a medieval painting of 'The Three Quick and the Three Dead'. Three kings in the prime of life, dressed in their pomp and finery, meet three skeletons: their own deaths striding towards them.

'Life's too short for all this nonsense; now you pull yourselves together, bury the hatchet, and make it up between the two of you!'

If that won't put a stop to their quarrel, nothing will.

The story of the stone hearts has worked its way into local legend. In fact the two stone effigies with their hearts in their hands are of William Gerbrugge (literally 'Yare Bridge') and his wife. He is remembered for building St Olave's Bridge over the River Yare near Haddiscoe. But why let the truth get in the way of a good story?

13

WILLIAM OF
THE STRONG HAND

It doesn't matter which direction Wymondham is approached from; it is always the church that draws the eye. It has two towers; one standing at the west end, the other at what would once have been the 'crossing'. The two towers bear testament to centuries of wrangling.

The church was founded as a Benedictine priory in 1107 by William de Albini. William was chief butler to Henry I, and his brother Richard was Abbot of St Albans. The Wymondham priory was founded as a 'daughter' of St Albans Abbey. All would have been straightforward if William hadn't also insisted that the church be made available to the townspeople as their place of worship. Unfortunately no directions were given as to which parts of the building should be used by whom … and a quarrel began which became so rancorous that in 1249 Pope Innocent IV felt obliged to intervene. He decreed that the town should have the nave, the north aisle and the north-west tower, and the priory should have the rest. Both factions raised new towers and hung new peals of bells. They were rung as gestures of defiance, town and priory trying to deafen each other with their devotions.

In the end, with the Dissolution of the Monasteries, it was the townsfolk who won the victory. The priory – by now designated as an abbey – fell into ruin, while the town's portion survived and is what we see today.

The pious William de Albini, who was buried before the high altar in Wymondham Priory in 1139, probably knew nothing of the discord he had set in motion. His home had been in Old Buckenham Castle where he had been married to Maud, the daughter of Bigod, first Earl of Norfolk. William de Albini and Maud had several children, but it is their eldest son, also named William, whose name lingers in both history books and folk memory.

After the death of Henry I, when Stephen had succeeded to the throne, the younger William de Albini courted the King's widow, Adeliza. He was by all accounts an attractive proposition, a sweet-talking courtier, a redoubtable warrior and a champion on the jousting field. She was smitten, and before long rings were exchanged and they were pledged to one another. A date for the wedding was set.

Meanwhile the Queen Dowager of France announced a tournament in Paris. All knights of mettle were invited, and William couldn't resist the challenge. To test his skills against those of the flowers of French accomplishment was a proposition too enticing to refuse. He immediately set sail for France. What he didn't know was that the Queen Dowager was looking for a new husband, and this tournament was designed to reveal him to her.

The assembled warriors were divided into two teams and they fell upon each other. The rules of a tournament in the twelfth century were few. The aim of the game was to dismount and capture as many of the opposing side as you could manage. The Queen sat on a raised platform, sipped wine, and watched the chaos. It soon became clear that one warrior excelled over all the others. She watched him toppling knights from their chargers, battering them with his blunted sword until they submitted, and then sending them to his pavilion with their heads bowed.

She raised her handkerchief and called a halt to the tournament. She asked that the warrior take off his helmet and come to the platform. And so it was that William de Albini, bloody and bruised, lifted his helmet and climbed the steps to her throne. He knelt before her; she set a crown of bright ribbons upon the sweating crown of his head and tied a jewelled collar around his throat. He kissed her hand. Trumpets sounded.

'Behold, the champion of the tournament!'

The Queen Dowager whispered, 'Will you join me for supper?'

He kissed her hand again: 'Madam, I would be honoured.'

But the supper he was offered was not the stately banquet he had expected. He was led up a winding staircase to a little room hung with tapestries. A table had been set for two. The Queen Dowager invited him to sit down.

Food was served and the doors were closed. They were alone. Soon, he felt her foot stroking his leg beneath the table. She smiled across at him.

'I am looking for a husband ... you are the man I most desire in all the world.'

William sprang to his feet.

'Madam ... it is not possible ... I am already pledged to another.'

Her eyes narrowed and her voice hardened.

'Then our meal is ended.'

She turned and disappeared through a door behind a tapestry. Servants led him out of her palace.

The next morning, he received a note from the Dowager Queen. He unfolded it and read: 'If you will not have me, then do me the courtesy of bidding me farewell. I will be in the royal garden after matins'.

William had little choice but to obey. He entered the royal garden. She had servants with her, but they fell away as he approached her. He bowed. She smiled.

'Ah good, you have come.'

She took his arm.

'Tell me, great warrior, William de Albini, is there anything in this world that frightens you?'

'It is not a manly quality to be afraid, Madam.'

'Not even of a lion ...?'

Suddenly he was seized from behind. He fought, but was quickly overwhelmed. He was dragged across the garden to a stone grotto. An iron grill was pulled open and he was flung inside. The grill clanged shut behind him. A hungry lion was growling and baring its teeth. Outside, the Dowager Queen stood with her arms folded, her head tilted to one side, watching him. Without a moment's hesitation William took off his cloak. He wrapped it around his right arm. He lunged forwards, thrust his hand into the lion's mouth, seized its tongue and tore it out. The animal fell to the ground, whimpering with pain.

William turned to the Dowager Queen, dropped to one knee and offered her the tongue on outstretched hands.

She ordered that the cage be opened. She took the bloody tongue, and with tears in her eyes told William to return to his English sweetheart.

The story travelled to England faster than William himself. When he reached Dover, Adeliza was waiting for him. She fell into his arms. They were married and she bore him seven children. From that day onwards he was known as William of the Strong Hand, and he assumed to bear, for his coat of arms, 'a lion gold in field gules'.

William lived a long and distinguished life. He fought for King Stephen during the Anarchy. He became the Earl of Arundel. He built the castle at Castle Rising. And when he died in 1176, his body was laid beside the body of his father before the high altar in Wymondham Priory.

14

THE WILD BOY

There has always been a fascination with the wild. Long after the great oak forests that once covered East Anglia had been felled, stories and superstitions about a race of wild men and wild women lingered. They were hairy, naked, forest-dwelling beings. They were almost human. They were creatures from before the Fall: innocent beings with the souls of animals. It was said that if you could get them drunk and bind them with ropes, they would exchange their wisdom for their freedom. Many Norfolk churches have images of these 'wodewose' – beings of the woods. Above the west door of St Agnes Church in Cawston, there's a carving of one fighting a dragon. There are several on the tops of buttresses at St Margaret's in Cley. There's one on the pulpit of St Andrew, Felmingham, and in a brass at St Margaret's in Kings Lynn, Sir Robert Braunche rests his right foot on a wodewose.

It's a fascination that has never waned. Stories of the Yeti, Bigfoot and feral children still capture our imaginations in a very particular way. The painted sign for the Wildman pub in Bedford Street in Norwich, which shows an almost naked boy with a bear to either side of him, commemorates a more recent wild man episode in Norwich's history.

In 1724, in the forests of Hertswold in Hanover, some peasants trapped a wild boy. He was naked, ran on all fours and could climb trees like a squirrel. He was filthy and baked brown by the sun, his hair was long and matted and his fingernails were like claws. He refused cooked meat, preferring to eat carrion and wild nuts and berries. He was estimated to be twelve years old. He spoke a language of hums, whinnies and grunts. The peasants claimed that the boy had been raised by bears.

King George I was fascinated by the wild boy. He had him brought over from Hanover to St James' Palace in London. For a while he became a sensation. He was wrestled into clothes each morning and presented at court where he giggled and howled and ran about, dipping his hands into the pockets of the aristocracy in the hopes of finding good things to eat. Daniel Defoe and Jonathan Swift wrote about him. There's a portrait of him at Kensington Palace, dressed in fine clothes, with a wild shock of curly hair and a satyr-like smile.

George I arranged for his education under Dr John Arbuthnot. He was baptised and given the name Peter. But the boy could learn nothing. He would not speak, read or write, though he loved to dance. He was described as having 'a natural tendency to get away if not held by his coat'. When Peter's behaviour got too out of hand he was beaten on the legs with a broad leather strap to 'keep him in awe'.

After a couple of years the court tired of the wild boy, and he was given to a farmer in Northchurch in Hertfordshire with a royal pension of £7 17s 6d per quarter towards his upkeep. There he was treated kindly, and he settled into life at the farm. He would load muck onto carts, but unload it again if not stopped. He was 'exceedingly timid and gentle in his nature'. He would eat raw onions as though they were apples. He liked a cup of gin. He was fascinated by fire and would sit on the hearthstone and stare into the flickering flames for hours at a time. If the night was clear, he loved to be outside beneath the stars. No one could persuade him to sleep in a bed. In the autumn he displayed 'a strange fondness for stealing away into the woods'. He always reappeared after a few days.

But then, in August 1751, when he was about thirty-nine years old, he stole away and didn't come back. No search party could find him. He seemed to have vanished.

In September of the same year there was a curious incident in Norwich. A 'sturdy vagrant' was arrested for 'strolling about the streets'. He had thick, bushy black hair and an enormous beard that was tangled with sticks and dead leaves. He was described as having a 'wild countenance and a very roving look with his eyes'. He was brought before a constable, who discovered that he could not speak. Either he made a deep humming sound or he neighed like a horse. The city authorities were unsure as to what to do with him, as he was guilty of no crime beyond begging for food. They decided to put him in the Bridewell Gaol. Safely locked away he wouldn't make a public nuisance of himself.

Then, on the night of 22 October 1751, a fire broke out in Bridewell Alley. It spread quickly from house to house, and soon engulfed the Bridewell Gaol. The inmates rattled the iron bars of their cells, coughing and choking, shouting to be set free. The turnkeys had no choice but to unlock the doors. Soon, thirty or so petty criminals had vanished into the smoky labyrinth of streets and alleys, while the local populace was struggling to put out the fire. With buckets and engines they hurled and pumped water into the flames. Suddenly, one of them noticed that the gaol wasn't quite empty. In one of the cells, its door wide open, a bearded figure was sitting watching the flames that were about to engulf him with a look of rapturous happiness on his face. With a shout, several brave souls ran into the gaol and dragged him to safety just as the blazing roof collapsed.

He was transferred to the parochial workhouse, but the drama of the fire had aroused a certain amount of local interest. One day a Norwich gentleman drew the overseer of the Bridewell Gaol aside and showed him an advertisement he had seen in the *London Evening Post*:

LOST, or stray'd away, from BROADWAY in the Parish of NORTH-CHURCH, near Barkhamstead in the county of Hertford, about three Months ago, PETER the WILD YOUTH, a black hairy Man, about five feet eight inches high, he cannot speak to be understood, but makes a kind of humming-Noise, and answers in that manner to the Name of PETER. Whoever will bring him to Mr Thomas Fenn's at the Place abovesaid, shall receive all reasonable Charges and a handsome Gratuity.

So Peter was returned to Hertfordshire, but not before a Norwich pub had been named in his honour with a sign showing him as a boy in his original German forest, with a bear parent to either side of him.

Mr Thomas Fenn had a brass collar made for Peter the Wild Youth, with his name and address engraved upon it so that he would never stray so far from home again. He lived happily until his master died. Then, he refused all his food and died shortly afterwards in February 1785. He would, by then, have been about seventy-three years old. His gravestone can still be seen in Northwich churchyard. The people of the parish had grown so fond of him that it was paid for by public subscription, and bears the inscription 'Peter the Wild Boy 1785'. Even today it is rarely without flowers.

15

TOM HICKATHRIFT

In the churchyard of the church of All Saints, in the village of Tilney All Saints, lies a long narrow stone. It's about 7ft long and broken in two places. It lies just beyond the eastern end of the church. It has been worn smooth by wind and weather, but it's said that years ago, carved into the stone, there was a circle with a cross inside it and beneath it a straight line.

The stone marks the grave of Tom Hickathrift, and it marks the end of a story that began many hundreds of years ago in the city of Ely.

In Ely, there once lived a man called Thomas Hickathrift. He was married to a ramping Ely girl called Joan. They had a son, and they called him Tom, after his old father. He grew up, and when he was old enough, he was sent to school. But Tom had no head for his ABCs or his 123s. All he wanted was to sit in front of the fire and warm his hands.

Old Thomas passed away, leaving poor Joan to raise the boy alone – and it wasn't easy. By the time Tom was ten years old, he stood 8ft tall in his stockinged feet. His hands were the size of shoulders of mutton, and he'd eat enough meat in one day to satisfy five full-grown men. His old mother had to work her fingers to the bone, and her bones to the marrow, to keep the boy alive.

One day she came into the parlour after a hard day's work, and saw Tom's enormous back hulking in the firelight. His great red hands were stretched towards the heat. He was whistling tunelessly between his teeth. Joan flew into a fury: 'Can't you do something useful, Tom! You're a waste of your time! You're a waste of my time! You go to Stamford's barn and fetch some straw for the floor of the house!'

In those days they had straw on the floors of their houses as we have carpets today. Tom lumbered to his feet.

'All right then, Mother.'

He ducked under the lintel of the doorway. He strode across the fields until he met Farmer Stamford: 'My old mother asked me to fetch some straw from your barn.'

'You take as much as you can carry, Tom.'

Farmer Stamford soon regretted his words. Tom went into the barn and piled stook upon stook until he'd got himself half a ton of straw. He roped it round and swung it onto his shoulder. Then he set off for home with the straw on his back, whistling all the way. Farmer Stamford stood and stared in astonishment.

From that day onwards there was no more hulking in the firelight for Tom Hickathrift. The story of his prodigious strength was out. Soon the world and his wife wanted Tom to work for them. At that time, there was a woodman living in Ely. He'd felled a mighty oak tree and he needed some help to lift its trunk onto a cart. He asked Tom and five other strong men to give him a hand. All morning Tom stood with his arms folded, and watched the five men as they set to with levers and winches – but the oak wouldn't budge. In the middle of the day, when he'd eaten his baggin and wiped the grease from his mouth with the back of his hand, Tom said: 'Stand you aside.'

He reached down, curled the fingers of one hand around the stump of a branch, lifted the trunk, swung it round, and lowered it onto the cart. The woodman was amazed.

'Well, Tom! What can I give you as payment for your trouble?'

'I'll tell you what,' said Tom, 'I'll have a twig for my old mother's fire.'

Beside the tree that had been felled was another still standing. Tom wrapped his arms around the trunk and heaved it out of the ground, roots and all. He lifted it onto his shoulder and set off striding across the fields towards Ely, whistling as he went.

It wasn't long before Tom Hickathrift was famous the length and the breadth of the Fens. At every fair, from Swaffham to Spalding, from Cottenham to Kings Lynn, he was a champion at the wrestling, boxing, tossing the cannonball, and all the other sports of the time. Even today, in a field in the parish of Terrington St Clement, a millstone lies half-buried in the ground that Tom is said to have thrown for a wager from the Tuesday Market place in Kings Lynn, some 6 miles away.

A brewer in Kings Lynn needed a man to bring barrels of beer from Kings Lynn to Wisbech. When he saw Tom Hickathrift at a hiring fair, he seemed to be the very man for the job.

'Now then Tom,' said the brewer, 'If you'll work for me, you can have as much beer as you can drink, as much meat as you can eat … and a new suit of clothes besides.'

That was payment after Tom's heart, and he readily agreed. The brewer told him how he was to lead his horses pulling the great brewer's cart, piled high with barrels, from Kings Lynn to Wisbech. Tom listened and nodded.

Now, at that time, between Kings Lynn and Wisbech, on the Smeeth – the great common that belonged to the 'seven towns of the

Marshland', Walpole St Peter, Walsoken, West Walton, Terrington, Clenchwarton, Emnett and Tilney – there lived a giant. He'd made his home in a cave on a low hill in the middle of the Smeeth. Tom Hickathrift stood tall, but this was a real giant. He towered as high as a house. His eyes were like barber's basins. His favourite sport was twisting the heads from his victims, and hanging them from the branches of an oak tree that grew on the top of his hill. All that was left of them he would devour, crunching their bones and licking their blood from his fingertips.

On account of this giant, the brewer gave Tom one last piece of advice: 'Now then Tom, when you lead the horses pulling my cart, don't take the short cut over the Smeeth. You go the long way, by road, d'ye understand?'

Tom nodded. 'All right then.'

The next day Tom started work, and for a few weeks, he did what he was told. But on his diet of strong meat and strong beer he grew stronger and bolder than he'd ever been before. One day, he was leading the horses out of Kings Lynn when he saw the track that led to the Smeeth. He thought to himself: 'Well, why not give it a try ... gain the horse or lose the saddle, as the saying goes ...'

He pushed open the gate and led the horses through.

When he came to the Smeeth, the giant nosed him. (A giant's nose is always more fine-tuned than his eyes or his ears.)

He came sauntering out of his cave, with a great gap-toothed grin stretched across his face. If there was one thing he loved more than human flesh, it was a barrel of ale.

'How now rogue, what brings you here so bold, in throwing open the gate and leaving the road? I'll make an example of you to all the rogues under the sun.'

He pointed to the spreading oak on the height of his hill. It was festooned, like a Christmas tree, with grisly trophies. Severed heads were hanging by their hair, some old with white bone jutting through blotchy blackened skin, some fresh with red blood dripping and dribbling still.

'D'ye see this tree? I'll hang your head the highest of them all!'

Tom reached under the back of one of the brewer's horses. He picked up a handful of horse-muck.

'You will, will ye?' he said, 'I'll tell you what … you can have a turd in the teeth for all your taunting talk!'

He hurled it and struck the giant's cheek. The giant bellowed with rage. He ran into his cave, and returned with a club in his hand as big as a mill-post.

'Here's the twig that'll make you see sense!'

He strode down towards Tom … and it was at that moment that Tom Hickathrift realised his mistake. He'd come without a weapon. All he had was the whip for driving the horses. He looked to left and right. There were no young trees he could pull up by the roots. What was he to do? Then, all of a sudden, he had an idea. He unharnessed the horses. He ran to the side of the brewer's cart. He curled his fingers under it and lifted. The cart toppled over and the barrels rolled across the ground. From the underside of the cart he snapped one of the iron axles. From the end of the axle he broke away the wheel. With the axle in one hand as a club and the wheel in the other as a shield, he stepped forward to the fight.

The giant brought his club swinging down through the air, but Tom jumped aside so that it caught the rim of his wheel and cracked it. The giant dropped to his knees with the strength of the stroke. Tom jumped into the air and gave him such a thwack on the side of the head with the axle that the giant was sent staggering left and right.

'What!' shouted Tom, 'Are you drunk on my strong beer already?'

Then they set to like hammer and tongs. All day they fought, making the hard ground soft, and the soft ground hard, with the fury of their fighting. By the end of the afternoon the giant was wet with sweat and blood.

'How now rogue,' he roared, 'let's have a little pause and drink some of that beer of yours.'

'I may be a fool,' said Tom, 'but I ain't such a dolt as all that.'

And he gave him another hefty whack. By the time the sun set, the giant was lying with his face in the grass, bellowing and begging for mercy. But Tom gave him no quarter. With the whip and the axle as noose and tourniquet he tore the giant's head from his shoulders. Then he fitted the axle and the cracked wheel to the cart. He pulled it upright, piled up the barrels and harnessed the horses. Soon he was leading them into Wisbech, whistling as he went.

The story of Tom's triumph spread like wildfire. The people of Wisbech lifted him onto their shoulders and carried him to the Smeeth. The people of the seven towns of the Marshland came swarming to their common. Sure enough, they found the giant's body ... and then they found his grimacing head. They lit a huge bonfire, and all that day there was feasting, dancing and celebration.

At the end of the day, when everyone had gone home, Tom ventured into the giant's cave. There he found, amongst a huge pile of gnawed bones, a great quantity of gold, silver and copper coins; the emptied pockets of the giant's victims. There was treasure enough to make him rich for life.

With the money, he paid for the building of a beautiful house called Hickathrift Hall. His old mother came to live with him. And from that day onwards, he was no longer known as Tom Hickathrift, but as Mr Thomas Hickathrift, gentleman.

It's said that years later he killed another giant, on the island of Thanet in Kent, and that afterwards the King himself dubbed him 'Sir Thomas Hickathrift'. It's also said that it's thanks to Tom that there are no lions, bears or wolves on British soil.

That's as maybe ... but what certainly is true is that, for all his strength and courage, Tom proved no match for old age. When he was 100 years old, and felt that his time had come, he hobbled out of his hall. A huge stone ball was lying on the ground.

'Wherever this ball falls, there you must lay my bones to rest.'

He gave it a tremendous kick. It flew through the air and cracked the east wall of Tilney church. Where the ball fell to the ground is where Tom is buried. Over his grave a stone was set. Carved into the stone were no words, for Tom had never mastered his ABCs. Instead, there was just a circle for the cartwheel and a straight line for the axle with which he'd fought the giant and saved the Smeeth all those years ago.

And Tom has never been forgotten. Throughout the marshland and the fens, if there's a dew-pond in a field, the chances are it'll be known as Tom Hickathrift's washbasin. If someone puts up a grandiose pair of gateposts, they'll be known as Tom Hickathrift's candlesticks. If a building is somehow in the wrong place (like the tower of West Walton church), it will have been lifted by Tom for a wager and put down slightly askew. If you want to catch a glimpse of Tom, you can go to Walpole St Peter; there's a small carving of him on the outside wall of the north chancel. But the best place of all is not in Norfolk at all: it's in Saffron Walden, where Tom and the giant are modelled in plaster on the outside gables of the Sun Inn, on the brink of doing battle.

16

MY SISTER, MY MISTRESS, MY MOTHER AND MY WIFE

Behind the organ in Martham Church is a memorial stone, bearing the inscription (carved in a pattern reminiscent of an hour-glass):

Here Lyeth
The Body of Christ.
Burraway, who departed
this life ye 18 day
of October, Anno Domini
1730
Aged 59 years
And there Lyes
Alice, who by hir Life
was my Sister, my Mistres,
My Mother, and my Wife.
Dyed Feb. Ye 12 1729
Aged 76 Years

The history behind the inscription is one that would have delighted the Greek tragedians. It is a true Norfolk tale that is worthy of Sophocles or Aeschylus – or, for that matter, Thomas Hardy – echoing the myths of the birth of Adonis and the marriage of Oedipus.

Alice, it seems, was the only daughter of a local tradesman or landowner; certainly a gentleman of some substance. When she was seventeen, she found that she had become pregnant by her own father, who had forced his attentions upon her against her will.

The double shame of a child conceived out of wedlock and an incestuous union caused her to conceal her pregnancy from the world. She feigned sickness, and the baby was born in secret. It's possible that a faithful servant or close friend had been taken into her confidence, and had helped with the delivery.

The baby was a healthy and beautiful boy ... but with one blemish. He had a large mole under his left shoulder blade. It was a mark that seemed only to enhance his beauty, and it was with an aching heart that she wrapped him in a soft blanket, put him in a basket, covered the basket with a cloth and took him by coach to Norwich, where she left him on the steps of the cathedral.

The years passed, Alice's father died, and she inherited his estate. She put her secret sorrow behind her. She had many suitors, being a handsome woman of property, but she couldn't bring herself to take a husband. She let herself be swept away by the demands of running a household and a business.

Twenty years later, she put out word that she needed a steward to manage the servants and the household accounts. A young Norwich man called Christopher Burraway presented himself at her house as an applicant for the post. Servants opened the door and led him to the parlour, where Alice was waiting to interview him. As soon as he entered the room she felt a strange, sudden, unexpected surge of attraction for this dapper and capable young man. He felt something similar, though all that passed between them were the usual formalities of question and answer, and the reading of references. She gave him the job. He was so good at it that she found she was able to let him take more and more responsibility for the household, allowing her to engage with her business interests. Before long, she became very prosperous.

Alongside the harmonious management of the estate came another harmony. Their attraction for each other deepened, and in time they became lovers. Because Christopher was of lower status than his mistress, their love affair had to be kept secret. Their clandestine trysts and liaisons, in linen-rooms, stables and pastures, were passionate but hurried. There was no time for lingering.

And then, to her surprise (she being nearly forty), Alice found that she was pregnant again. All social distinctions were cast aside, and to the amazement of the household and the local gentry, she and Christopher announced that they were to become man and wife.

On their wedding night, they undressed to go to bed. He leaned forward to pick up his nightshirt, and in the flickering candle-light, she noticed a mark beneath his left shoulder blade. She gasped. He turned to her.

'What's troubling you?'

'Turn your back to me again.'

She lifted a candle and touched the mole with the tip of her finger.

'Who were your parents?'

'William and Elizabeth Burraway … I have told you before. Good people, God rest their souls, who treated me kindly, though I was not their own.'

'How did you come into their household?'

'They found me on the cathedral steps, and having no babes of their own, they took me as a son.'

Alice threw herself onto the bed, buried her face in her hands, and shook with sobs. He dropped beside her and held her in his arms. She turned to him, her face wet with tears:

'You are my son. My lost son. My lost, forgotten son who has come back to me … and now I find that I am married to him.'

She told him her story. When she had finished, he put his hand gently upon hers.

'Nobody need know; no soul need know of this. It is our secret, for as long as either one of us draws breath. Only in death will the world know our story … and until the time comes for our tombstone to be carved, we shall be man and wife as any other.'

17

EDMUND, KING AND MARTYR

Between Hunstanton and Old Hunstanton is St Edmund's Point. It's a stretch of 'striped' cliff showing layers of carstone, red chalk, and white chalk. On the cliff-top is a ruined chapel that is said to mark the place where East Anglia's greatest king first set foot upon English soil.

The legend tells us that King Offa of East Anglia had no sons. On a pilgrimage to Jerusalem he visited his cousin, King Akmund of Saxony. He was deeply affected by his cousin's youngest son, Edmund, and decided to make him his own adopted son and the heir to his throne. On the journey home from the Holy Land, Offa was passing through Constantinople when he fell ill and died. On his deathbed, he pulled his coronation ring from his finger and told his noblemen to take it to Saxony and put it onto Edmund's finger as a token of his will.

So it was that, in AD 854, Edmund sailed to the promised Kingdom of East Anglia with a company of noblemen. He was fourteen years old. When he reached St Edmund's Point (then called Maydenbure), he dropped to his knees and kissed the ground, praying to God to bless his coming. When he stood up, seven springs of sweet water burst out of the ground. From that moment, the soils of North Norfolk became rich and fertile and bore the richest crops in East Anglia.

From Hunstanton, Edmund journeyed to Attleborough, where he spent a year in contemplation, learning the psalms by heart. On Christmas Day AD 855 he was crowned King of the North Folk by Bishop Humbert of North Elmham. A year later, he was made King of all East Anglia.

There followed ten golden years of peace and prosperity. Despite his youth, Edmund is said to have ruled his kingdom with strength and justice. He was a protector of widows and orphans, a benefactor to the poor, an upholder of justice and a defender of the church. It is said that during those ten years, a slave-boy could drive a mule-drawn cart piled high with treasure from Lynn to Ipswich, and not one coin would be stolen from him. Edmund is described as being tall and broad-shouldered with long flaxen hair and a large hooked nose. When he wasn't worshipping or fulfilling his kingly duties, he delighted in hunting in the oak woodlands that still covered much of East Anglia. He divided his time between his royal seats or 'vills' at Hunstanton, Attleborough and Caister in what is now Norfolk, and Bures and Rendlesham in Suffolk.

But to tell Edmund's story we must leave him for a while, and travel across the North Sea to Denmark.

While Offa was still ruling over East Anglia, there was, in Denmark, a woman of legendary beauty. Her name was Thora. She had had many suitors, but her virginity was protected by a yellow venomous snake. Any man who approached her with love in his head, or his heart, or his loins, would be attacked by the snake. It would sink its poisoned fangs into his thigh and he would die a slow and agonising death. Many men had attempted to win her, and all of them had perished.

But there was at that time a nobleman called Ragnor, who was determined to win the hand of the proud and beautiful Thora. He killed a wolf. From the wolfskin he made himself a pair of breeches. He smeared the fur of his breeches with thick, sticky, black pitch. Then he approached her. The yellow snake slid through the grass, and sank its fangs into the pitch and fur. Ragnor drew his knife and killed it. Thora fell into his arms. From that day onwards, he was known as Ragnor Lodbrok – Ragnor Hairy-breeks.

The years passed, and Ragnor and Thora were happy. They had two sons, called Ubba and Inguar. Their sons grew up into fine young men. And then one day, possibly in the late summer of AD 864, Ragnor Lodbrok was out hunting close to the sea's edge. Bounding beside him was his favourite hunting dog, a great black wolfhound. On his wrist he was carrying a speckled falcon. Suddenly he saw a flock of white geese flying overhead. He unhooded his falcon and it flew up into the air. It swooped and sank its talons into the neck of one of the geese. The two birds plummeted down into the sea. There was a great creaming of the water with their wings, but neither bird rose up again.

On the beach was a little boat. Ragnor dragged it over the shingle and into the water. He jumped into it, his dog beside him. Soon he was rowing out across the waves to rescue his speckled falcon, and to wring the neck of the goose. But out of nowhere a storm came. It drove his little rowing boat, spinning and tossing, across the North Sea like a leaf carried by the current of a raging river. For three days and nights, Ragnor was swept up in the storm. He was driven across the water to the coast of East Anglia, blown up the estuary of the River Yare, and finally thrown up onto the mudflats at Reedham.

The next morning, when the storm had stilled and the sky had cleared, the people of Reedham saw a little boat washed up on the mud. They waded out to look at it. They peered inside. Lying on the bilge-boards they saw a man and a dog, both sodden and half-dead with exhaustion. The people of Reedham lifted and carried them to one of their low reed-thatched cottages. They stripped the stranger of his clothes, and wrapped him in blankets and skins. They lay the man and dog before the fire, and pressed sops of milk-soaked bread into their mouths. They knew the stranger was no peasant by the finely-worked cloak clasp they had unfastened from his shoulder. Slowly man and dog regained their strength. When they were strong enough, the people of Reedham brought them to their king.

King Edmund was holding court at Caister. When the tall stranger with the black dog loping at his heels was brought before him, he invited the stranger to sit down at the mead-bench. As a Christian, he was pledged to help those in need; and besides, there was something about this nobleman from across the water that he found himself warming to. The people of Reedham told their story, and then Ragnor Lodbrok spoke. The Saxon and Danish languages were close enough for him to make himself understood. He told the story of the great storm. Edmund listened. He offered the stranger mead, bread, meat, cheese and honeyed cakes. Soon, Edmund and Ragnor were talking as though they were old friends. Edmund invited Ragnor to stay as his guest at Caister.

Day followed day. The English king and the Dane enjoyed each other's company. They went out hunting. It soon became clear that Ragnor was a finer huntsman than any of Edmund's men. He was swifter of foot, quicker to fit an arrow to a bowstring, stronger in the thrusting of a boar-spear ... and his dog was fleeter and bolder than any of Edmund's dogs.

At that time Edmund's chief huntsman was called Bern. Every day, Bern saw his own skill being undermined by the greater skill of this stranger from across the water. He saw how Edmund sought

Ragnor's advice rather than his own. A bitter, yellow, bubbling bile of jealousy began to well in the pit of Bern's belly.

Then, one clear winter's day, Ragnor and Bern were hunting together in an oak forest. Ragnor was ahead of Bern; his black wolfhound was bounding between the trees. Suddenly Bern was overwhelmed by bitter envy. He couldn't control himself. He fitted an arrow to his bowstring, drew it back and loosed it. It struck Ragnor between the shoulders. He dropped to his knees. Bern drew his dagger. He seized the Dane by the hair, pulled back his head and cut his throat. He buried Ragnor in a shallow grave in the forest, and covered the fresh earth with dead leaves.

That night in the feasting hall at Caister, there was no sign of Ragnor Lodbrok. Edmund turned to Bern: 'Where's the Dane?'

Bern shrugged: 'I don't know. We were hunting in the forest. We separated. I never saw him again.'

The feast continued and Ragnor did not appear. But at midnight, a strange thing happened. There came a sudden sound of scratching and scraping at the doors of the hall. When they were opened, Ragnor's black wolfhound ran into the hall. It ate the scraps of food that had fallen onto the floor under the feasting table, then turned and ran back out into the night.

Night followed night and Ragnor did not return, but always at midnight the wolfhound scratched at the door, ran into the hall, ate the scraps and vanished into the darkness. On the fourth night, King Edmund decided to follow Ragnor's dog. When it had finished eating and turned to run out of the hall, he leapt over the feasting table and followed it. The dog ran through the doors, across the compound, across the fields and into the forest. There was a clear full moon shining overhead. Edmund followed the dog between the trees. When it came to a low mound of earth and dead leaves it threw itself down, rolling its head from side to side and howling.

Edmund crouched, and pushed his fingers into the soft earth. He dug with his hands, and soon felt the cold, smooth skin of a corpse against his fingertips. He pulled the body of Ragnor from its shallow grave. He rolled it over. Between the shoulders was an arrow that he recognised instantly. It was one of Bern's arrows. He lifted the body of his friend tenderly in his arms, and carried it to Caister. The dog followed, with its tail curled up between its legs. Bern was dragged from his bed and bound with chains. Ragnor's body was laid out on the feasting table with candles burning at its head and feet.

The next day there was a funeral. Ragnor, though he had been a worshipper of the Norse gods, was given a Christian burial at Caister. The black wolfhound watched its master's body being lowered into the ground, and then turned and sloped away into the forest.

When the funeral was finished Edmund summoned his advisers, his ealdormen, to decide the punishment that Bern should suffer for his crime. As Christians, they agreed that the fate of Bern should be left to the will of Almighty God. They decided that he should be stripped of all his clothes, put into Ragnor's little boat without food, drink, sail or oars, towed far out to sea and left to the mercy of the waves.

So Bern was unchained. Stark-mother-naked he was thrown into Ragnor's boat and towed out into the North Sea, beyond sight of land. But the will of God is inscrutable and beyond the measure of mortal minds. The little boat was carried by the waves and currents of the sea. For three days and nights it was driven by the winds, and washed up on the coast of Denmark.

When the people of Denmark saw that Ragnor's boat had returned, they were amazed. They ran down to the shingle beach and peered inside. There was a man lying on the bilge-boards, naked and half-dead with exhaustion. They lifted and carried him to one of their reed-thatched huts. They wrapped him in blankets and skins, and pressed soft food into his mouth. When he was strong enough, they gave him clothes to wear and led him to Ragnor's wife Thora, and his two sons Ubba and Inguar.

Thora looked the stranger up and down: 'Who are you? Where have you come from? What were you doing in my husband's boat?'

Bern, who wanted to get his revenge on Edmund for the punishment he had received, answered: 'Listen, I have a terrible tale to tell. Your husband Ragnor Lodbrok was driven across the sea by a sudden storm, and washed up on the coast of East Anglia. He was brought before the king of that country, King Edmund.'

Bern spat onto the floor.

'Your husband begged for mercy and safe haven, but Edmund would not listen. He ordered that an iron cage be constructed. He ordered that Ragnor be put inside it. He ordered that a great bonfire be built. He ordered that the cage be thrown into the flames. And when your husband had been burned to black ashes, he ordered that those ashes be scattered over a dunghill. Such is the charity of the Christian god he worships.'

Thora threw herself onto the ground. She buried her face in the dust and wept. But her two sons, Ubba and Inguar, thrust their hands into the fire that blazed in their mother's hall and swore an oath by all their gods; by Odin, Thor, Freyr, Balder, Heimdall, Tyr and Loki. They swore that they would be avenged 10,000 times for the death of their father. When they drew their hands out of the flames, they were blackened and blistered. But it had been their left hands, not their sword hands, that they had burned.

All winter the Danes made preparations. In the spring of AD 865 a fleet of dragon-prowed ships, under the leadership of the two brothers, set sail. But the winds blew them off course. They landed at the estuary of the River Humber. All that summer they drove inland, slaughtering and pillaging until it was said that in the northeast of England not one stone was left standing on another, and the furrows of the fields ran red with spilt blood. At the first chill of autumn, the Danes returned to their ships and sailed homewards.

All the next year, they made preparations. The following spring they sailed again. This time, their ships landed at Weybourne, and soon they were fighting their way into East Anglia. Edmund's army met the Danes in many frenzied battles. Some of the earthworks that his men are said to have dug are still visible to this day: Bunn's Bank near Attleborough and the Devil's Dyke (sometimes called St Edmund's Dyke), that runs across Newmarket Heath between Wood Ditton and Reach.

Finally, Edmund's army was surrounded by the Danes in one of his fortress stockades. Some say it was at Old Buckenham, others that it was at Framlingham in Suffolk. Either way, the Danes laid siege for many weeks. Provisions ran lower and lower, until all that Edmund's men had left to eat were one bull and two sacks of grain. Edmund dropped to his knees and prayed for guidance. Suddenly an idea entered his mind. He said to his men: 'Tighten your belts and feed all the grain to the bull.'

They did as they were told. Soon, they were weak with hunger and the bull was sleek and fat.

'Now', said Edmund, 'open the gates and set the bull free.'

His men looked at him as though he had lost his wits, but he was their king, so again they did as they had been told. They opened the gates of the stockade and the bull ran out, trumpeting and snorting.

When the Danes saw the bull they shouted: 'Look! Here's meat for a feast!'

One of them hurled his spear and brought the bull crashing to the ground. Soon, it was skinned and butchered. But as they were dressing the carcass, they pulled out the bull's stomach. It was swollen and heavy. They were surprised and showed it to their leaders. Ubba held the bull's stomach in his left hand, took a dagger from his belt and slit it open. The choicest grain trickled down onto the grass at his feet.

'We have been laying siege to this place for months ... and still they have grain enough to feed the best of it to their cattle. This siege could last forever.'

Already the first frosts of winter were whitening the ground. Ubba and Ingmar ordered their men to return to Weybourne. They then sailed home to Denmark.

But all the next year they made preparations, and in the spring of AD 869 they sailed for the third time. A tremendous fleet of ships landed at Orford. This time, the Danish army split into two halves, with Ubba leading one half, Inguar the other. They drove far inland. They sacked the monasteries of Peterborough, Crowland, Thorney and Ely. Norwich was sacked and burnt to the ground.

Finally, Edmund's army met Ubba's army at Thetford. All day the battle raged. By the time the sun set, it was clear that Edmund had won a tremendous victory. As the moon climbed into the sky, Edmund's exhausted men lit fires and nursed their wounds. But there came the sudden sound of battle horns. Inguar's army fell upon the tattered remnant of Edmund's men and as the sky brightened with stars there was terrible slaughter.

When dawn broke on the morning of the 20 November, Edmund saw Bishop Humbert making his way through the carnage of the battlefield; he was leading a horse.

'Edmund, my king, you must flee for your life, muster another army, reconquer this land for Christ.'

But Edmund had seen too much bloodshed. He shook his head.

'O Humbert, my father, rather I should die than the whole nation perish.'

He climbed up into the saddle, but he didn't gallop from the battlefield; instead he rode slowly, with his head bowed in sorrow. The Danes saw him and followed. He rode to a place called Haegelisdun. Some people claim that Heigelisdun is Hoxne in Suffolk, others that it is Hellesdon to the north of Norwich. He entered a church and prostrated himself before the altar. The Danes surrounded the church. Ubba and Inguar entered, and seized the man they believed to be their father's murderer. They dragged him outside and tied him to an oak tree. They beat him with the flats of their swords and whipped him with flails. Edmund called unceasingly on the name of Jesus Christ. This drove the brothers to a frenzy of rage. They ordered their archers to loose arrows at Edmund, but to aim with such care that none of his vital organs were to be pierced. Soon Edmund was pinned to the tree by more than 100 arrows. In the Anglo-Saxon chronicles he was described as looking more like a hedgehog than a man. But still he was alive, and still he called on the name of Jesus Christ.

Finally, Ubba drew his sword and hacked off Edmund's head. He kicked it among the bushes. And the two brothers, triumphant at having subdued East Anglia and avenged the death of Ragnor Lodbrok, ordered their men to return to their ships at Orford.

As soon as the Danes were gone, the people of East Anglia searched for their king. Soon they found his body, pinned to an oak tree by 100 arrows. They pulled out the arrows and laid the corpse on a stone slab. Then they searched for his head. For three days they searched far and wide, but could not find it. Then they heard a voice:

'Here! Here!'

It was coming from a tangle of brambles.

'Here! Here!'

They parted the brambles and they saw a wonder. Ragnor's enormous black wolfhound (more wolf than hound), gone feral in the oak forests, was crouching with Edmund's head between its paws. And Edmund's lips were moving:

'Here! Here!'

One brave soul came forward and lifted the head. The wolfhound showed no anger. As soon as the head had been taken, it got slowly to its feet and quietly disappeared among the trees.

The head was carried to where the body lay. It was set to the shoulders, and straight away the skin of the neck melted and melded until there was only a thin red line to show that they had once been separated. The body was buried. Edmund's grave became a place of miracles, so much so that the story of his death reached Rome, and he was pronounced a saint and canonised. The body was exhumed. It was found to be uncorrupted, as though Edmund was merely in a deep sleep. It was taken to a place where a vault could be constructed for it. Over the vault a shrine and a monastery were built. That place is called Bury St Edmunds to this day.

And as for Bern the hunter, it is said that he lived the rest of his life in Denmark, honoured among the Danes. But when he died his soul went, straight as a plumb line, down to Hell.

And it's said that the great black wolfhound who saw the death of his master, and the death of his master's friend at the hands of his master's two sons ... it's said that that dog still runs wild in Norfolk and Suffolk, and one glimpse of him presages ill fortune and bad luck. His name is Black Shuck.

Edmund is celebrated all over Norfolk. There are images of him in churches at Martham, Outwell, Knapton, Barnham Broom, Catfield, Litcham, Ludham, Stalham, Trimingham and Norwich

Cathedral, to mention but a few. It's rumoured that it was the shock of his death that inspired Alfred of Wessex to lead his armies to victory over the Danes.

For a while, Edmund was England's patron saint, until he was usurped by St George, who never even set foot on English soil. In East Anglia he has never been forgotten, and there are many people who are convinced that the time is ripe for him to be reinstated.

18

OLD SHUCK

North-east of the church of St Mary in Southery (built in 1858) is the ruin of the old church. On the north side of the old church ruin the charnel house used to stand, and its stone foundations can still be seen – gnawed away by what seem to be tooth-marks.

When the old church was built by order of the Abbot of Ely, the parish of Southery was still untamed fen, and its inhabitants were as wild as their landscape. So the builders were given a pack of wolfhounds for their protection. Unfortunately the dogs didn't like the fish they were given as food, preferring the sweeter meat of the monks they were supposed to be protecting. When their supply of monks ran out they began to kill and eat each other, until only the fiercest and most cunning of the pack was left alive – a bitch as big as a donkey.

One harsh winter a Southery man found the bitch half-dead from starvation. With the help of some villagers he carried her to his turf-walled, reed-thatched hut. His wife had recently given birth to a baby and she had milk to spare, so she offered her breasts to the dog, who drank thirstily and regained her strength.

Soon the wolfhound became tame and the fenmen would take her poaching on the high ground, and often enough she would bring them venison from the Baron of Northwold's deer parks, which made a welcome addition to their accustomed diet of eel and gruel.

Then one day the great bitch vanished. When she returned, the pads of her feet were torn, as though she had made a long journey … and her belly was swollen with pups.

The monks, who had resumed their work on building the church, this time under armed guard, looked at her and shook their heads. 'It is the Devil's work,' they said, and made the sign of the cross whenever they saw her.

At last she whelped in a dark corner of the hut of the fenman who had saved her. She had one puppy only. When it first crawled out into the light, villagers and monks gathered in amazement – it was enormous, as black as night, and its eyes were bright red.

The puppy grew to be the size of an ox. Like its mother, it hunted for the villagers of Southery, and like its mother it cast a baleful, hungry eye on the monks (though it was well enough fed to spare them). But the reputation of its kind would catch up with it in the end. When the church was finished and the Bishop of Elmham came to consecrate it, one of the monks, who was a survivor of the first batch of builders and had seen his brothers attacked and eaten, saw the dog. When he clapped eyes on this wolfhound the size of an ox, he shuddered and made up his mind to kill it. But before he could seize a bow and fit an arrow to the bowstring, the dog, sensing danger, leapt at him and tore out his throat. The Bishop's men wasted no time; soon arrows and spears were whistling through the air, and the dog, howling terribly, crawled into the fen to die.

But even though he's dead, the dog is not gone. He wanders the fens still, sometimes coming to the charnel house of Southery Church and gnawing at the stones to try and reach the bones inside. And if you glimpse him on 29 May (the date of the Southery Village Feast), you can be sure you'll be dead before the feast comes around again.

In 1857, Lord and Lady Lothian of Blickling Hall brought the architect Benjamin Woodward to design a new 'morning room'. An old woman of the village said to the parson: 'I wish these young people would not pull down the partitions.'

'Why so?'

'Oh, because of the dog.'

She was referring to an almost-forgotten story. One of the owners of Blickling Hall had been so unspeakably evil that when he died, he could not be buried in consecrated or common ground. The earth spat him out and refused him. Finally, his body was weighed down with stones and thrown into Blickling Lake.

A week later, a keeper was fishing in the lake and he landed an enormous eel. It was taken to the kitchens of the hall and laid on a dish to be prepared for the table. Whilst it was still writhing and gasping on its platter it vanished, and in its place lay a black dog with the dead man's eyes. It leapt from the table and bounded up the stairs into the hall. No one could trap it. It roamed the house and grounds, and from the moment of its appearance, ill fortune descended upon Blicking Hall. The dead nobleman's son and heir sickened with smallpox, the head keeper killed himself, the cook went mad, the milk turned sour and the crops were blighted.

At last a 'cunning man' was brought up from London. He whistled seven times, and at the seventh whistle the dog came fawning and grovelling at his feet. He led the dog to the south-east turret and threw in an ox bone. The dog sat and chewed whilst a village stonemason bricked up the door.

Peace returned and the curse was lifted. The estate passed to other families and the story was almost forgotten. But then, one summer evening in 1857, the three daughters of Lord and Lady Lothian were in the nearly completed 'morning room'. Suddenly one of them said: 'Look! Did you see it? That dog.'

The next morning, Benjamin Woodward and Lord Lothian were breakfasting together. The architect, who knew nothing of the story or the events of the evening before said: 'By the way Sir, yesterday I had the old turret opened. It had been bricked up, I suspect, for several hundred years.'

On the night of 28 January 1709, there was a terrible storm in the North Sea. Waves as high as churches crashed onto the shingle and rushed headlong into the marshes, tearing down trees and buffeting the houses of Weybourne, Salthouse, Cley and Blakeney. Caught in the storm was the Whitby brig *The Ever Hopeful*. She was travelling from London back to Yorkshire with a cargo of tea, wine and spices, but she would never reach her destination. Caught in pitch darkness in the lashing, crashing breakers she lost sight of the beacons on Cromer and Blakeney church towers and came too close to land. She was driven onto the shallow shoals off Salthouse and began to break up. The crew could see the beach barely twenty yards away … but between them and dry land was a surging, sucking white maelstrom of water. Wave after wave broke over *The Ever Hopeful*, tearing at spars, timbers and masts and whipping away the rigging. There was no choice for the crew but to jump and pray.

The next morning, when the storm had eased, their bodies were found washed up on the shingle. No one had survived. The cargo too was scattered along the length of Salthouse shore. There were those who carried the dead to Salthouse Church for Christian burial, and there were those, less scrupulous, who salvaged what they could of the flotsam and jetsam before the excise-men arrived on the scene. And there were those (least scrupulous of all) who made sure that none of the dead went into the ground with golden rings on their fingers or in their ears.

But as the dripping, bloated corpses were being lifted and loaded onto carts, a strange discovery was made. One of them, the ship's captain, judging by the cut of his coat, had his swollen fingers curled inside the collar of a great drowned mastiff. The dog's jaws were clamped to the captain's jacket. It was as though the dog had been trying to drag his master to safety, and the master had been dragging his dog.

It was enough to put a quietness on any man. The people of Salthouse gathered round the two corpses. Then, with hushed whispers, they gently eased the fingers from the collar and pulled the coat from between the jaws.

The dog was buried on Salthouse beach; the captain, with his crew, in an unmarked mass grave in Salthouse churchyard.

But within weeks of the shipwreck, the ghost of the dog had been seen running and howling along the road between Salthouse and Cley. It was searching for its lost master. Its eyes were red with weeping, and it was the size of a calf. Its coat was shaggy and black as the night.

The dog still runs that stretch of coast. He is most often glimpsed at the end of January, and when there is a storm at sea his howls can be heard mingling with the roaring of the wind. There are those, though, who say the story is told mostly by smugglers, who want the honest burghers of Cley and Salthouse to stay indoors while they're at work.

These are three origin stories for the Black Dog who haunts Norfolk (the Edmund story offers another). One glimpse of him is supposed to presage ill fortune. There have been many accounts of sightings. His most common name is Shuck – it is thought to derive partly from the Old English word 'scucca' meaning a devil or goblin, and partly from the dialect word 'shucky', meaning shaggy or unkempt. He's also been called 'Hateful Thing', 'Skeff', 'Owd Rugman', 'Galleytrot', 'Old Scarfe', and 'Padfoot'.

Descriptions of him all run on similar lines. Here's an example from Geldeston:

They du speak of a dog that walks regular. They call him Skeff and his eyes are as big as saucers and blaze wi' fire. He is fair as big as a small wee pony, and his coat is all skeffy-like, a shaggy coat across, like an old sheep. He has a lane, and a place out of which he come, and he vanish when he hev gone far enough.

Most chilling are the many little anecdotes that continue to be told to the present day.

A Bawburgh man was cycling home after a darts match. By the village signpost he saw the biggest hound he'd ever set eyes on, with eyes that shone like coals of fire. He sped up and cycled past him, but soon heard the hound approaching from behind, the pads of his paws beating the grit road. The dog passed the bicycle, so close the rider could smell his rankness, then stopped in the middle of the road and turned. The man dismounted, not knowing what to do. Suddenly a car with no headlights, clearly driven by a drunk, careered along the road towards them. He flung himself and his bike into a ditch. When he climbed out the dog was still standing in the road, unharmed. It turned and vanished into thin air. Though he thanked Old Shuck for saving his life that day, within a couple of years his wife had sickened and died.

I'll give the last word on Shuck to a certain Mr Finch of Neatishead. He was walking in the road after dark and saw a dog, which he thought was Dick Allard's, which had snapped and snarled at him on several occasions. The dog was running straight towards him. He thought: 'You've upset me two or three times, I'll upset you now. You won't turn out of the road for me, neither will I for you.'

Along came the dog in the middle of the road. Finch gave him a hefty kick … and his foot went through him as it would through a sheet of paper.

19

COCK AND BULL

During the sixteenth and seventeenth centuries, especially during the turbulent reigns of Henry VIII and Charles I, there was a national obsession with prophecy. Cryptic pamphlets were published, and cryptic rhymes spoken, that foretold the destiny of nations. Attributed to Merlin or Mother Shipton, they spoke a riddling language involving strange creatures and surreal circumstances. Sceptics of the time dubbed them 'cock and bull stories'. The term has lingered even if the prophesies have been forgotten.

Merlin, whose strange prophecies were published in 1652, seems to have been obsessed with the north Norfolk coast, particularly Weybourne. Perhaps this isn't surprising, as the unusually steep shingle bank there provides easy landing for invaders. The Vikings are said to have beached there, and the seafront was fortified against invasion at the time of the Spanish Armada, the Napoleonic Wars and the Second World War. This was what Merlin had to say:

The proudest prince in all Christendom shall go through Shropham Dale to Lopham Ward, where the White Lion shall meet with him in a fight in a field at South Lopham, were the prince aforesaid shall be slain under the minster wall … Then there shall come out of Denmark a Duke and he shall bring with him the King of Denmark and sixteen great lords … they shall land at Waborne Stone, they shall be met by the Red Deere, the Heath Cock, the Hound and the Harrow. Between Waborne and Branksbrim (Brancaster), a forest and a church-gate, there shall be fought so mortal a battle, that from Branksbrim to Cromer Bridge it shall run blood. Then shall the King of Denmark be slain and all the perilous fishes in his company. Then shall the duke come forth manfully to Clare Hall where the bare and headlesse men shall meet him and slay all his lords … and chase his men to the sea where twenty thousand of them shall be drowned without dint of the sword. Then shall come in the French King, and he shall land at Waborne Hope, eighteen miles from Norwich: there shall he be let in by a false mayor …

Mother Shipton foresaw a similarly apocalyptic destiny for Norfolk, but it was to be the east rather than the north coast that would suffer:

England shall be won and lost three times in one day … there is to come a man who shall have three thumbs on one hand, who is to hold the King's horses in battle; he is to be born in London and be a miller by business. The battle is to be fought at Rackheath Stone Hill, on the Norwich road. Ravens shall carry the blood away, it will be so clotted. The men shall be killed, so that one man shall be left to seven women, and the daughters shall come home and say to their mothers: 'Lawk, mother, I have seen a man!' The women shall have to finish the harvest. The town of Yarmouth shall become a nettle-bush … but blessed are they that live in Potter Heigham and double-blessed them that live in it.

Curing the reign of Henry VIII, prophecies of this kind were believed so sincerely by the common people, and excited so much alarm, that an Act of Parliament was passed declaring that 'If any person should print, write, speak, sing or declare to any other person any such False prophecies of arms, fiends, beasts, fowls or such-like things, they shall be deemed guilty of Felony, without benefit of the clergy'.

We get a glimpse of the suggestive power of these prophesies during Kett's rebellion of 1549. The rebels, protesting against enclosure, set up camp on Mousehold Heath. It was a huge encampment, more than 20,000 strong. Within weeks, the rebels controlled the city of Norwich. On 24 August the Earl of Warwick, with an army of German mercenaries, came to suppress the uprising. The rebels held a favourable position on the high ground of the Heath. But there was a prophetic rhyme that had been on the tongues of Ketts' men:

> The county Gnoffes, Hob, Dick and Hick
> With clubbs and clowted shoon
> Shall fill the vale
> of Duffin's dale
> With slaughtered bodies soon.

When Kett's army saw the Duke of Warwick's soldiers in Dussindale (an area of Thorpe St Andrew), they were beguiled by the prophecy to forsake the heath and come down into the river valley to risk battle on open ground. The result was disaster. As a historian of the time put it:

> They came into the valley believing themselves to be the upholsterers that were to make Duffin's Dale a large soft pillow for death to rest on, whereas they proved only the stuffing to fill the same.

As to the prophecies of Merlin and Mother Shipton: they haven't happened yet, but who knows? ... maybe we should be keeping a weather-eye open for Heath-cocks, Hounds and Harrows, for Perilous Fishes and Men with Three Thumbs ... and if we see them, maybe we should all up-sticks and move to Potter Heigham.

20

TOM PAINE'S BONES

There is a long tradition of dissent and radicalism in Norfolk. The stories of the dissenters, while not strictly folk tales, have become the stuff of legend.

A mile south of North Walsham, the remains of a medieval stone cross beside the B1150 mark the site of the battlefield where Jack Litester, a dyer from Felmingham known as the 'King of the Commons', was defeated by Henry de Spencer in June 1381. Litester was the leader of the Norfolk strand of the Peasants' Revolt. A combination of heavy taxation and a corrupt land-owning clergy had driven the impoverished commoners to challenge the authority of church and state. After his defeat he was hanged, drawn, and quartered. The four quarters of his body were displayed in Norwich, Kings Lynn, Yarmouth and Felmingham. His followers were butchered in St Nicholas' church in North Walsham, where they were seeking sanctuary.

Beside the old Norwich Road between Wymondham and Hethersett stands the iron-hooped remnant of an ancient oak tree. It marks the place where Robert Kett and his followers swore a solemn oath to reform the abuses of the state and put an end to enclosure. Kett, a landowner, having seen local men pulling up his fences, had ridden out to confront them, but was so convinced by their arguments that he ended up helping them to destroy his own enclosures. He soon found himself at the head of an army of 20,000 supporters on what is now called Kett's Hill on Mousehold Heath in Norwich. He commanded his troops from a platform among the branches of another great oak that was christened 'the Throne of Reformation'. The rebellion was defeated and Kett was hanged from the wall of Norwich Castle. There is now a plaque on the castle wall:

IN 1549 ROBERT KETT YEOMAN FARMER OF WYMONDHAM WAS EXECUTED BY HANGING IN THIS CASTLE AFTER THE DEFEAT OF THE NORFOLK REBELLION OF WHICH HE WAS THE LEADER. IN 1949 FOUR HUNDRED YEARS LATER THIS MEMORIAL WAS PLACED HERE BY THE CITIZENS OF NORWICH IN REPARATION AND HONOUR TO A NOTABLE AND COURAGEOUS LEADER IN THE LONG STRUGGLE OF THE COMMON PEOPLE OF ENGLAND TO ESCAPE FROM A SERVILE LIFE INTO THE FREEDOM OF JUST CONDITIONS.

It was a struggle that was still being fought 300 years later by George Edwards. Like many radicals of the nineteenth century, Edwards was a Nonconformist; a Primitive Methodist, a 'Ranter'. He was born into utter poverty in Marsham. At five years old he worked from dawn to dusk as a bird-scarer. He was paid a shilling a week, and when he was found curled up asleep between the furrows, he was whipped and fined tuppence. His father was discovered with five stolen turnips and was sacked and fined 5s. The family was forced into the workhouse. These were the early scars that drove Edwards – who had never been to school – to learn to read, to educate himself, and to campaign against rural poverty. In 1906, aged fifty-six, he founded the Eastern Counties Agricultural Labourers' Union in the Angel Hotel in North Walsham. It would become the National Agricultural Workers Union. When he was in his late fifties he cycled 6,000 miles in Norfolk enlisting men to the union, often speaking to big crowds in open fields as no farmer would allow him access to shelter. As an old man he became the first Labour Party MP for South Norfolk. He had to borrow a suit from his Tory opponent to be allowed into the House of Commons.

But the greatest Norfolk radical of them all was Thomas Paine. His golden statue can be seen in Thetford town centre. He was born there, the son of a corset-maker. For the first thirty-seven years of his life he lived and worked in Norfolk and Sussex. He was deeply affected by the preaching of John Wesley and in 1774 he sailed for America, a place of 'infinite possibility, where the world can begin afresh'. He'd been encouraged to visit by his friend Benjamin Franklin. He immediately began to campaign against the slave trade, and he wrote a pamphlet called 'Common Sense' in which he encouraged the Americans to throw off the shackles of 'his Mad-jesty and the No-ability' and seek a true democracy. The pamphlet became a rallying call for the American War of Independence. Tom Paine called on the Goddess of Liberty to come down from the heavens and overthrow the King of England.

> A fair-budding branch from the gardens above
> Where millions with millions agree
> She brought in her hand as a pledge of her love
> And we called the plant 'Liberty Tree'
>
> In the shade of that tree, like the fathers of old,
> Our bread in contentment we ate,
> Unvexed by the troubles of silver and gold
> Or the cares of the grand and the great.

From the east to the west blow the trumpet to arms
Through the land let the sound of it flee,
May the far and the near all unite with a cheer
In defence of our Liberty Tree.

Soon every town had its 'Liberty Tree', festooned with bright ribbons, and many of the flags that fluttered in the wind during the great battles of the American War of Independence carried its image. When the war was over and America had achieved her independence, it was Tom who coined the phrase 'The United States of America'.

Then, he sailed back to England and wrote his treatise the *Rights of Man*, in which, alongside his usual tirade against inherited wealth and power, he outlined a plan for the welfare state that was nearly 200 years ahead of its time.

He was described as being a 'wicked, malicious, seditious person, ill-disposed to His Majesty and the happy government of His realm'. Warrants were issued for Tom's arrest. So he slipped across the English Channel to France where he was given a hero's welcome as a 'Friend of the Revolution'. He threw in his lot with Robespierre. But as the French Revolution became more and more bloody, and King Louis XIV and Marie Antoinette were condemned to death, he began to campaign for moderation. He argued, 'It is the office of kingship, not the officer, that is at fault.'

Robespierre took this as a betrayal. Tom Paine was imprisoned and condemned to the guillotine. While he was languishing in a prison cell in Paris, he fell into a fever. He asked one of the gaolers to open the door of his cell so that a cooling breeze could blow onto his face. The gaoler, seeing Tom's weak condition, took pity on him. The door was opened wide. It was at that moment that marks were made on the doors of every cell in which the occupant was to be executed. The mark was made on the inside of Tom's door, due to it being wide open and flat against the wall.

When the time came for the condemned to be dragged to their deaths, Tom's door had been closed again. He was saved. A little while later, Robespierre fell from power and Tom was pardoned.

He lived in Paris for many years. He met Napoleon, who told him that he always slept with a copy of the *Rights of Man* under his pillow, and also that a golden statue of Tom should be set up in every city in Europe. There's only one – and that's in Thetford.

When he was an old man, Tom decided to return to America. But while he had been living in Paris, he had lost his religious conviction. He had written a book called *The Age of Reason* in which he ridiculed the church and the Holy Scriptures, arguing that: 'If we want to know what God is, we should not go to those scriptures that could have been written by the hand of any man. We should go, rather, to that scripture that is creation itself.'

Benjamin Franklin was appalled. He and the other founding fathers turned their backs on Tom, and would have nothing to do with him. He was forced to live out the last of his days in abject poverty. When he died he was given a pauper's funeral. Soon his grave was a tangle of brambles and briars.

Poor Tom Paine, there he lies,
Nobody laughs and nobody cries,
Where he's gone to, how he fares,
Nobody knows and nobody cares.

But then, thirty years later, one of a new generation of English radicals, William Cobbett, was travelling in America. He was an admirer of Tom Paine, and visited his grave to pay his respects. He was appalled to find that it was unkempt and overgrown. He returned in the dead of night with a spade, and dug up Tom's bones. He put them into a sack and carried them across the Atlantic and back to England.

Nobody knows what William Cobbett did with the bones of Tom Paine. Maybe, on one of his famous 'Rural Rides', as he was passing through East Anglia, he buried them among the roots of Kett's famous oak, 'The Throne of Reformation', the original Norfolk Liberty Tree. Maybe he held back a few bones to plant under Jack Litester's cross. We'll never know. But certainly the *Rights of Man* would have been among the books that George Edwards, having been taught to read in his mid-twenties by his wife Charlotte, would have soaked up avidly.

21

THE GREEN LADY

In 1894 a member of the Folklore Society, W. B. Gerish, heard this story from a ninety-five-year-old Norfolk woman. The old woman's name is not given, nor where she came from, but she claimed to have heard the tale 'a score o' times'. It is a wonder-tale, a 'once upon a time' story; not rooted in time or place, but certain details give it a Norfolk flavour: the word 'dob' for 'curtsey' and, especially, the gooseberry patch. No Norfolk cottage garden would have been without one. I've taken Katherine Briggs' suggestion and adapted the end of the story using its sister-tale, 'The Three Heads in the Well' as a source.

Once upon a time there lived a poor old man who had three daughters. One day the eldest daughter said: 'Father, give me a cake and a bottle of water so that I can go and seek my fortune.'

Her father gave her what she asked for and she set off along the road. After a while she met a little old man who asked her: 'Where are you going?'

'To seek service.'

'Give me your cake and water, then walk 'til you see a house with a green door. Knock and you'll find fortune … though whether for good or ill I cannot tell.'

The girl replied:

> The road is long, my legs ain't strong
> I'll keep my cake and water.

She walked for a long time, eating and drinking as she went, until she came to the house with a green door. She knocked at the door. Out came a lady who was green from head to foot. Her hair, her face, her dress, her hands, and her feet were as green as leaves, and her two eyes as green and sharp as emeralds.

'What do you want?'

'I've come seeking service.'

'What can you do?'

The girl made a dob (curtsey).

'I can bake and I can brew, and I can make an Irish stew.'

The green lady looked her up and down.

'Very well, I'll take you on, but on two conditions: You must neither look up the chimney nor inside the clock-case of the grandfather clock.'

The girl agreed and they went inside. That night, she slept in front of the fire. The next morning she was up at the crack of dawn, cleaning and washing the hearth. As she was working, the green lady's daughter came down the stairs. She was as green as her mother and she was riding a black cat.

'Be so kind as to cut me a slice of bread and spread some butter on it.'

The girl turned.

'Can't you see I'm scrubbing the hearthstone?'

'Then you'll scrub no longer!'

She called upstairs, and her mother came riding down with a chopper in her hand. With one swing of it the girl's head was cut clean from her shoulders. The green daughter hung the head in the chimney, and her mother put the body in the clock-case of the grandfather clock.

Some little while later, the second daughter set off to seek her fortune with a cake and a bottle of water. She met the little old man and all happened as before:

> The road is long, my legs ain't strong
> I'll keep my bread and water.

When she came to the house with the green door she made a dob: 'I can bake and I can brew and I can make an Irish stew.'

The green lady took her on with the same two conditions. The next morning the girl was up at the crack of dawn, cleaning and washing the doorstep. Down came the green daughter on her black cat.

'Be so kind as to cut me a slice of bread and spread some butter on it.'

'Can't you see I'm scrubbing the doorstep?'

'Then you'll scrub no longer!'

Down came the green lady with a chopper in her hand, and with one swing of it the girl's head was cut clean from her shoulders. The head was hung in the chimney, and the body in the clock.

Well, weeks and months passed. Then, one day, the youngest daughter set off to seek her fortune. After she'd walked for a while she met the little old man: 'Where are you going?'

'To seek service.'

'Give me your cake and water, then walk 'til you see a house with a green door. Knock and you'll find your fortune … though whether for good or ill I cannot tell.'

The girl replied:

The road is long, my legs are strong
Please take my bread and water.

She walked for a long time, her belly aching with hunger, until she came to the house with a green door: out came the lady, green as leaves and her eyes as sharp as emeralds.

'What do you want?'

'I've come seeking service.'

'What can you do?'

She made a dob.

'I can bake and I can brew, and I can make an Irish stew.'

'Very well, I'll take you on, but on two conditions, you must neither look up the chimney, nor inside the clock-case of the grandfather clock.'

The third daughter said neither yes nor no, but followed the green lady into the house. That night she slept in front of the fire. The next morning she was up at the crack of dawn, cleaning and washing the oven. Down came the green lady's daughter: 'Be so kind as to cut me a slice of bread and spread some butter on it.'

The girl jumped to her feet and fetched a loaf from the cupboard. She sliced and buttered it, and gave it to the green daughter. The daughter was delighted. She called to her mother, and all three of them sat at the table and ate their fill … and as for the girl, she ate and ate until her aching belly ached no longer.

That afternoon, when the oven had been cleaned spotless, the green lady said: 'You stay and mind the house; we're going out for a ride.'

The two black cats were saddled and bridled, and the green lady and her daughter rode away across the green fields and into the green woods.

As soon as they were gone, the girl ran to the chimney and looked upwards. There, she saw the heads of her two sisters hanging by their hair. She reached and took them down. She sat with them cradled in her lap. She combed their hair and washed the soot from their cheeks with her tears.

Then she looked in the clock-case of the grandfather clock. There, she saw her sisters' bodies. She pulled them out and laid them on the ground. She straightened the folds and creases of their skirts and blouses. Then she put their heads to their shoulders. And the skin of their necks melted and melded, and their eyes winked and blinked, and each of them drew in a breath of air.

'Where have we been?'

'Never mind that', said the third daughter, 'Quick! Come with me!'

She took their hands and they ran out into the garden. They ran past apple and pear trees until they came to a clump of gooseberry bushes. The girl called out:

> Hide us hide us
> So that they won't find us
> If they do they'll break our bones
> And bury us under the marble stones.

They dived in among the bushes, and not one thorn pierced them. They were only just in time. The green lady and her daughter came riding up to the house. They opened the door.

'Be so kind as to cut us a slice of bread and spread some butter on it.'

But there was no answer. They looked here and there. The girl was gone. They looked up the chimney and inside the clock. Her sisters were gone. They shrieked with fury. They seized their choppers and leapt onto the backs of the two black cats.

First they asked the apple trees: 'Where did they go?'

But the apple trees wouldn't answer, so they chopped them down.

Then they asked the pear trees: 'Where did they go?'

But the pear trees wouldn't answer, so they chopped them down.

Then they came to the gooseberry patch.

'Which way did they go?'

And one gooseberry bush said: 'This way and that way and hither and yon.'

And another gooseberry bush said: 'And on and over the river.'

So they rode out of the garden to the river's edge, and they whipped the black cats into the water … but down they sank and the water closed over them. The green lady and her daughter were drowned.

As for the three sisters, they crawled out from under the gooseberry bushes, went to the house, lifted the latch and opened the door. They searched downstairs and upstairs, they peered into chests and cupboards … and they found gold enough to last them the rest of their days.

So they lived happy, and so may we, let's put on the kettle and have a cup of tea.

22

ANNE BOLEYN

The night of 19 May is a busy one in Norfolk. At Blickling Hall, a headless coachman whips four headless horses to a gallop, whilst inside the carriage a woman sits demurely with her severed head in her lap. At Salle Church, a weeping hare squats on an unlettered black marble slab. And on the path outside Blofield Church, two noblemen fight with swords of fire.

All of these spectral visions are part of the same story. It's a story that begins in Salle. In the floor of the church there is a modest brass to Geoffrey Boleyn and his wife Alice. They were local farmers who capitalised on the wool trade that flourished after the Black Death. Their son became wealthy enough to purchase Blickling Hall from Sir John Falstoff, the prototype for Shakespeare's Falstaff. Their grandson Thomas, a respected mercer with a talent for languages and diplomacy, married Lady Elizabeth Howard and was appointed Earl of Wiltshire.

Thomas and Elizabeth Boleyn had three children: George, Mary and Anne. Their childhood years were spent at Blickling Hall, and then, as teenagers, the two girls were sent to France as ladies-in-waiting to the Queen of France (Henry VIII's sister). It was on their return that the sisters, with their French dress and style, were noticed by the King. Mary briefly became Henry's mistress, but her sister played a more dangerous and beguiling game. Anne was quick-witted and effervescent, and although never recognised as a great beauty, she had a powerful sexual allure that the King found irresistible. But she was careful to withhold her favours until Henry had broken from Rome, divorced Katherine of Aragon and made her an offer of marriage.

On 25 January 1533, they were declared husband and wife. Later that year she gave birth to a daughter, Elizabeth. The King was besotted with Anne Boleyn. It was said that she was the only woman who ever dared to argue with him or answer him back. She was feisty and passionate, and with her ascendancy, the Boleyns became one of the most powerful families in England. Her brother George was made Lord Rochford and appointed to the Royal Privy Chamber.

But, despite their rise to power, the Boleyns were no more than local farmers made good. Their wealth was what would later be termed 'new money'; there was more good fortune than blue blood coursing in their veins. The real Norfolk aristocrats were the Pastons. One of them, Sir Thomas Paston, was a courtier to Henry VIII. And as he watched Anne's coquettish, teasing game with the King, bringing the upstart Boleyns into prime positions of power, he was consumed with a bitter and obsessive jealousy. He watched and waited for his moment.

He didn't have to wait long. The birth of a healthy daughter was followed by the miscarriage of a son. The foetus of the lost child was said to be malformed. By now the King was beginning to tire of Anne, and he was desperate for a healthy son and heir. He was overheard whispering to a courtier, 'I made this marriage, seduced and constrained by sortileges (sorcery).'

Thomas Paston struck. He spread scandalous stories about Anne in the Royal Court. He let it be known that her powers of seduction had not only been directed at the King, but at five of his courtiers: Sir Francis Weston, William Brereton, Mark Smeaton, Sir Henry Norris and – most scandalous of all – her own brother Lord Rochford. He claimed that the misshapen, miscarried child was the incestuous love child of Anne and her brother. He claimed that Anne and her lovers had been plotting the King's death. And he claimed that Anne had indeed 'constrained the King by sortileges' and was a witch.

It didn't take long for the tittle-tattle to reach the ears of the King, and although there were proven grounds for believing only one of the allegations, he saw that they offered him a way out of an irritating marriage. The five courtiers were brought to trial, and with the help of some excruciating torture, were found guilty and executed. And Anne herself, the Queen of England, was condemned to death.

At eight in the morning on 19 May 1536, dressed in a robe of black damask covered by a white ermine mantle, Anne Boleyn was blindfolded and then beheaded by a French swordsman. As a traitor she was entitled to neither funeral nor proper burial; her body was put into an elm box that had once contained bow-staves and was placed in a communal grave in the Chapel of St Peter ad Vincula in the Tower of London.

But though the story might end there, the legend doesn't. It is said that the poet Sir Thomas Wyatt (who had also been accused of having sexual liaisons with Anne, but had been acquitted) used his influence to retrieve the body from its resting place in the Tower. It was taken to his house in London and embalmed, and then given into the safe keeping of Thomas Boleyn, Earl of Wiltshire: Anne's father.

Thomas had arranged for a grave to be opened in Salle Church, the ancient burial place of the Boleyn family. The body was secretly carried back to Norfolk.

In his *Bentley's Miscellany*, Charles Dickens tells the story:

> What the Earl's thoughts and reflections were during the two hours
> he was unobservedly travelling by Aylsham and Cawston to Salle,
> it would not be difficult to divine. He had within a month lost a
> daughter and a son by the hand of the executioner – that son his only
> son – that daughter the Queen of England. Her name, besides, had
> been branded with infamy … the bitter reflections of those two hours
> perhaps the better prepared the Earl for the solemn ceremonies that
> awaited his coming at Salle Church. He alighted there at Midnight.
> A few faithful servants bore the mangled remains of his daughter to
> the side of her tomb … One priest was there, and the few candles that
> were lighted did no more than show the gloom in which they were
> shrouded. But all that could be done for the murdered queen was
> done – mass was said for the repose of her soul – De Profundis (Psalm
> 130) was chanted by those present – her remains were carefully
> lowered into the grave, where they now rest, and a black marble slab,
> without either inscription or initials, alone marked the spot which
> contains all that was mortal of Anne Boleyn - once Queen of England.

The one accusation made by Thomas Paston against poor Anne
that had some possible grounding in truth was the one that, to a
modern sensibility, seems the most unlikely. It was the accusation of
witchcraft. Anne Boleyn had an extra finger to her left hand, and, it
was whispered, a third breast – the vestigial trace of a nipple beneath
her right breast. In the sixteenth century, this would have served as
proof of witchery. And there were mutterings that Anne had been
seen suckling a little familiar in the shape of a hare at her third breast.
Whatever the truth or untruth of the allegation, it is a hare that can
be seen squatting on the black marble stone in Salle Church on 19
May; a weeping hare that waits until the last chime of midnight
and then bounds down the aisle and vanishes among the shadows
beneath the tower.

At the same time, Anne herself returns to Blickling Hall, the
place of her childhood; headless, and driven by headless horses and a
headless coachman.

But what of the duel at Blofield with swords of fire? That is the duel that was fought between Thomas Boleyn, Earl of Wiltshire, and Thomas Paston, Duke of Norfolk. Seeking revenge for the savage unfounded rumours and the deaths of his daughter and son, Thomas Boleyn challenged Thomas Paston, and they crossed swords on the path that leads from Blofield Church (St Andrew and St Peter) to St Michaels at Braydeston. It seems the duel was inconclusive and both men survived, but on the anniversary of Anne's death they are condemned to fight it again with swords of fire, year upon year, to the end of time. When one man is overcome, the ground swallows him, while the other vanishes into thin air.

As for the Boleyns: within a year of Anne's death her mother Elizabeth died, it is said, of a broken heart. Thomas Boleyn survived her by only a few months, and Mary died in 1542. The Boleyn dynasty had come to an end. But let's not forget that Elizabeth Tudor, Anne's daughter, one of the greatest monarchs to grace the English throne, had a quarter of her blood from good, shrewd, Norfolk farming stock.

23

THE DAUNTLESS GIRL

In the church of St Margaret at Stratton Strawless is the tomb of Thomas Marsham. He is dressed in his shroud and below him, through a grate, we can glimpse a carved charnel house, the bones neatly stacked. Until the Reformation most churches had charnel houses, where, according to Francis Blomfield, human remains were brought 'if dry and clean from flesh, there to be decently reserved until the last day … the bones piled in good order, the skulls, arms and leg bones in their distinct rows and courses'.

It is a crypt of this kind, tidily stacked with bones, that we need to imagine in the tale of the Dauntless Girl.

There was once a farmer, and he was sitting in his parlour sharing a bottle of the best French brandy with a couple of friends. When the bottle was empty he called his maidservant: 'Mary, go down to the cellar and fetch another bottle.'

Mary came to the door: 'I would if I could, Sir, but you've just drained the last we have.'

'Then go down to the inn and buy one.'

He threw his purse to Mary; she caught it, curtsied, and closed the door. The two friends turned to the farmer.

'You can't send her out on a night like this.'

'A slip of a moon, lowering cloud, and all the lanes awash with puddles ... and a good mile's walk there and back in nought but pitch blackness.'

The farmer shrugged.

'Young Mary, she's afeard of nothing, whether it be living or dead.'

He threw a log onto the fire and stretched his feet towards the flames. Half an hour later, Mary was back with the bottle.

'What did I tell ye?'

When their glasses had been filled several times more, the farmer opened his purse and pulled out a guinea. He set it on the table.

'I'll lay a wager. I'll meet you here in one week's time, and I'll bet you this golden guinea that you can't name a task that my Mary won't do.'

One of his friends shook his head.

'She's but a slip of a girl, and pretty besides. I'll have nothing to do with it.'

But the other shook the farmer's hand.

'You're on.'

Six days later, he paid a visit to the sexton: 'Tomorrow night I want you to hide in the charnel house and put the wind up young Mary. I'll pay you half a guinea for your trouble.'

The sexton had a terror of the charnel house, but half a guinea was 10s 6d, so he agreed.

When they met next evening, the farmer's friend said: 'Here's what Mary won't do. I'll wager she won't go alone to the church at midnight, go down the stone steps to the charnel house without candle or taper, and fetch me a skull bone.'

The farmer called Mary, and told her the task. The dauntless girl shrugged. At half past eleven she pulled on a warm coat, opened the door and vanished into the night. At half past twelve, she was back. She came into the parlour and put a skull down onto the table.

The farmer's friend looked at it and shuddered.

'Didn't you hear anything, Mary?'

Mary looked at him and smiled: 'Funny you should mention it … yes I did … I went down the stone steps without a candle or a taper, and I reached about with my hands 'till I felt the smooth pate of a skull, and I was just liftin' it up when some fool of a ghost says, 'Let that be, that's my father's skull bone'. So I put it down and picked up another and the ghost says, 'Let that be, that's my mother's skull bone', so I picked up a third and he says, 'Let that be …' but I'd had enough by then and I told him straight: 'Father or mother, sister or brother I must have a skull bone' … and here it be!'

The farmer's friend opened his purse, pulled out a golden guinea and gave it to the farmer. The farmer gave it to Mary, and she dropped it into her pocket.

'Oh, and one thing more. As I was leaving the charnel house, I saw the glint of a key in the door, so I closed the door and turned the key. And as I climbed the stone steps didn't the old ghost start a-hollering and a-shrieking … but I paid him no mind.'

The next morning the sexton was found, face down on the dusty floor of the charnel house, stone-cold dead with fright.

The story of the dauntless girl travelled from village to village, and reached the ears of a squire. Now this squire had recently buried his old mother … but she wouldn't rest. Every day her ghost wandered the house, and at mealtimes she'd sit down at the table and the servants would see her knife and fork lift up and play about as though she was eating. It was too much for them. One by one, they gave their notice and left the place, until the poor squire found himself alone with only a ghost for company.

The squire went to the farmer.

'I understand you have a maidservant who's afeared of nothing, whether it be living or dead.'

'I have.'

'Well, if she'll come and work for me, I'll double her wage.'

Mary overheard him and wasted no time. She packed up her few bits and pieces, and travelled home with the squire. That evening they sat down to supper. The door opened, the sound of footsteps crossed the room, the chair pulled back of its own accord, and the knife and fork began their dance. Mary served up a plate of mutton and vegetables, and put it at the ghost's place at table.

'Salt, Ma'am?' she asked, 'Pepper, Ma'am?'

Every night it was the same, and when she laid the table, Mary was always careful not to set the knife across the fork, in case the sign of the cross might frighten the ghost away.

And then, one day, the squire was away in London. Mary was cleaning the parlour grate. Out of the corner of her eye she saw a thin thing push through the parlour door. It was the old woman's ghost, and this time she could see it as clear as day, though it was of no more substance than a sea-fret or a ground mist. The ghost whispered.

'Mary, are you afeared of me?'

'No, Ma'am, I've no call to be afeared of you, for you are dead and I'm alive.'

'Mary, you're a good girl and you've treated me kindly … now if you'll follow me down to the cellar, I'll show you something to your advantage.'

Mary fetched a candlestick, but the ghost shook her head.

'No need of a candle Mary, I'll shine enough to light your way.'

So they made their way down the steps to the cellar, Mary following the ghost, who shone as bright as any lantern. The ghost pointed to some loose tiles on the floor.

'Pick up those tiles, Mary.'

She did as she was told, and she saw that underneath there were two bags of gold, a big one and a small one.

'The big one is for your master, Mary, and the little bag's for you, for you are a dauntless girl and you deserve it.'

And with those words the ghost vanished, and poor Mary had a deal of trouble finding her way out of the cellar and up the steps in the pitch black darkness.

A few days later the squire returned from London.

'Well then Mary, how have you and the ghost been rubbing along together?'

And Mary said, 'If you ain't afeared to come down into the cellar, I'll show you something special.'

And the squire raised his eyebrows, for Mary was a pretty girl, as well as a quick one.

'I'm not afeared if you're not afeared.'

So they lit a lantern and went down.

'Here are two bags of gold that your mother showed me ... and the little one's for you and the big'n's mine.'

The squire was a little taken aback that his mother hadn't left him the big bag ... but he was so smitten by the dauntless girl that he bit his tongue and said nothing.

And that evening, Mary crossed the knives and forks to keep the ghost from telling the truth of the matter ... but she needn't have worried, for the very next day the squire dropped to his knees and asked her for her hand in marriage – and she agreed.

And so there was a wedding and they both got both bags ... and if they haven't spent the gold yet, then they're spending it still.

24

SEAFARERS

Thirty miles north-east of Yarmouth is Smith's Knoll. It was, at one time, one of the richest fishing grounds in Europe. Between September and the end of November a fleet of 1,000 ships filled Yarmouth harbour. It was said that you could cross the River Yare from one side to the other, stepping from deck to deck. They were all pursuing the same fish; the 'silver darling', or herring. It has been estimated that at the height of the herring fishing industry, between 1870 and 1915, 60 million herrings might be caught in a single day off Yarmouth and Lowestoft. As many as 400 million might be caught in a season.

They were sold fresh, they were salted in barrels, and they were smoked, both as kippers and as 'red herrings'. The red herring, according to the Elizabethan writer Thomas Nashe, was invented in Yarmouth:

> A Fisherman of Yarmouth, having drawan so many herrings he wist not what to do withall, hung the residue that he could not sel ... in the sooty roof of his shad a-drying ... the weather was cold and good fires hee kept ... and what with his fiering and smoking ... in his narrow lobby, his herrings, which were as white as whales bones when hee hung them up, now lookt as red as a lobster ... and when hee and his wife espied it ... they fell down upon their knees and blessed themslvs and cried 'A miracle, a miracle!'
>
> And with proclaiming it among their neighbours they could not be content, but to the court the fishermen would, and present it to the King, then lying at Burgh Castle two mile off ... Saint Denis for Fraunce, Saint James for Spaine, Saint Patrick for Ireland, Saint George for England, and the Red Herring for Yarmouth.

All along the Norfolk coast, the sea has provided a livelihood. Kings Lynn was once one of the great British seaports. In the medieval period vast quantities of wool, grain and salt were exported through the port of Lynn; wax, timber, wine and furs were imported. Some of the huge Hanseatic storehouses can still be seen off King Street.

In the eighteenth century, whaling ships sailed from Norfolk to Greenland. Whale oil would fetch 30s a ton and the streets of London were lit by it. One Norfolk whaler, James Bartley, while trying to harpoon a whale, fell into its mouth and was swallowed. When the whale was finally killed, its stomach was opened, and Bartley was found inside, still alive. But from that day onwards, because of the whale's juices, his skin was wrinkled and a deathly grey-white colour.

All along the Norfolk coast crabs, cockles, shrimps, lobsters, oysters, lampreys, sprats, cod and herring have always been part of the local diet, and salted, smoked or frozen, have been marketed the length and breadth of Europe.

The old Norfolk fishermen knew the North Sea intimately. Colin Elliott has written:

> ... they could set a course ... from memory and sail it with an instinctive built-in allowance for lee-way and tidal set. In thick fog they would make a safe land-fall after negotiating tortuous channels which only allowed a narrow safe passage in a vast expanse of open water. They sailed with an intimate knowledge of the changing colour and surface pattern of the sea which told them where they were in 600 miles of watery waste. Above all they knew the shape of the bottom of the sea like other men knew the bumps and dips of their back gardens ... They were ship-handlers whose skill will never again be matched, and the sort of navigation they practised is now all but a lost art.

But the sea is a fickle mistress. One day she can be bright and tranquil, then the next her grey, crashing breakers will be throwing corpses up onto the sand. It's no wonder that sailors are a superstitious breed. In Norfolk it was considered bad luck to sail on a Sunday or to set out on a voyage on a Friday. To mention a pig or to carry money on board ship was dangerous, as was allowing a woman to cross the gangplank. Any glimpse of a monk, a nun, a priest or a cross-eyed person before setting sail was hazardous. To stick a knife into the mast invited a gale from the direction the handle was pointing. To learn how to swim was to make a death by drowning more likely. But most hazardous of all were mermaids.

A Norfolk trawlerman told the folklorist Ruth Tongue how, when he was a boy, his grandfather had once told him a story about a mermaid ... and all his uncles had got up and quietly left the room. They were fishermen and even to hear the word spoken was considered dangerous. His grandfather, though, had retired from the sea and having had a few drinks, felt at liberty to tell his story.

He told how he had once sailed northwards from Yarmouth, up the eastern coast of England to Scotland. He had been on one of two trawlers that were sailing together, both under the command of one owner. The fishing started well, but got better and better the further north they journeyed. They were hauling in net after net of fish. The men began to grow uneasy. It was as though something was luring them on with all this wonderful fishing. The owner was delighted with the catch. He laughed at their qualms and told them to keep working.

Then they saw something ahead of them, drifting on the tide. It was the broken wreck of a ship, floating aimlessly on the water. And there was something sitting on the timbers. As they drew closer, they saw it was a mermaid. They tried not to look at her but she drew their eyes like a lodestone. She was beautiful, pale-skinned, and red-lipped, with long green hair like sea kelp.

The grandfather pulled a clasp-knife from his belt. As soon as he felt cold iron against his skin, the mermaid's allure was broken. He shouted to his shipmates to do the same. They came to their senses.

'Pull for land!'

The ship swung round and headed for the nearest port. But the other trawler had the owner on board, and he was bewitched by the mermaid's glamour. He couldn't take his eyes off her. He ordered his men to sail closer and closer.

The grandfather's boat came into Dunbar harbour, and no sooner had they tied her fast than a storm broke. The other trawler was never seen again.

The trawlerman who told the story said that he'd asked his grandfather for the same story a few weeks later.

'What story?'

'The one about the lost boat … the one about the mer –'

But before the word had been completed, his grandfather had pulled off his belt and given him the first lick of a thrashing.

It's not surprising that Norfolk has produced two of the greatest seafarers in English history: George Vancouver and Horatio Nelson. Neither of them seems to have been troubled by superstitious fear … or by any fear at all.

The story is told of Nelson who, as a child had gone bird-nesting with some village boys from Burnham Thorpe. He'd wandered off on his own and when supper was served at the Parsonage, there was no sign of him. His family, worried that he might have been stolen by gypsies, set off in search of him. After a while they found him sitting quietly on the far side of a river that he'd been unable to cross. He was brought home. When he'd been fed and warmed by the fire, his grandmother asked him: 'Horatio, I wonder that hunger and fear did not drive you home.'

To which the future hero of the battle of the Nile, Copenhagen and Trafalgar answered: 'Fear! I never saw fear – what is it?'

Nelson went to sea at twelve years old on a ship called the *Raisonnable*. At fourteen, on a voyage of discovery to the North Pole, he secretly left the ship. He was sighted by one of the crew, fighting a polar bear with the butt end of his musket. It had failed to fire at the critical moment. The ship shot a cannon and the great bear lumbered away. Nelson was brought before the captain and asked why he'd ventured out on such a hazardous adventure. He answered: 'I wished to lure the bear, that I might take its skin home to my father in Burnham Thorpe.'

Throughout his career, Nelson returned again and again to Norfolk. He declared, 'I am a Norfolk man, and glory in being so.'

After the Battle of the Nile, he docked in Great Yarmouth. He was greeted by a vast crowd, cheering wildly and firing gun salutes into the air. When he stepped into his carriage, the horses were removed from the shafts and the people drew him through the streets to The Wrestlers' Arms, where he was granted the freedom of the borough. After the ceremony, the landlady, Mrs Suckling, asked permission to change the name of the Inn to The Nelson Arms. Nelson looked at her and smiled.

'Maybe not Madam,' he said, 'being that I have but one.'

George Vancouver grew up in Kings Lynn. He went to sea when he was fifteen, in 1762. He sailed with Captain Cook to Australia, and charted the coastline of Van Diemen's Land (Tasmania). He mapped Jamaica, and then, in an epic four-year expedition, mapped the north-west coast of North America from San Francisco to Alaska so accurately that the charts were still being used more than 100 years later. Vancouver Island was named after him.

Such exploits are the result of thousands of years of cumulative knowledge, the 'mysteries' of sea-craft passed from generation to generation, from the Saxon and Viking master-mariners to the present day. Most of the local knowledge has been carried by unlettered men, working shoulder to shoulder in the fickle reaches of the North Sea. Here's Bob Roberts, skipper of the last sailing barge to work the coast of East Anglia. He's writing in 1960, but it could have been 200, 400, or 600 years earlier:

> One winter's night we mustered from Greenhithe to Norwich with wheat, just as darkness was closing in. There was a strong south-west wind which had been blowing for several days; not a gale, but rough and blustery. By the time we were down Sea Reach several cloths of the mainsail had to be brailed up to ease the helm and she streaked off down the West and East Swin channels with a wake like a packet-boat. Before daylight we were off Yarmouth pierheads, having run 114 miles in fifteen hours …

25

THE GREY GOOSE
FEATHER

Years ago, in the Fens, there was a secret society called 'The Brotherhood of the Grey Goose Feather'. If any fen-man (or fen-woman) was in danger or needed help, if he'd been initiated into the society, he only had to show a grey goose feather with a split stem and he'd be helped without question.

In the last days of the English Civil War, Charles I – 'Charlie Wag' as he was known in Norfolk – was on the run from Oliver Cromwell, or 'Old Nol'. On 30 April 1646 Charles was sheltered by Sir Ralph Skipwith at Snowre Hall, 3 miles to the south of Downham Market. The King needed to cross the fens to Huntingdon, where one of his men would be waiting at the Bell Tavern to lead him to the Royalist stronghold at Oxford. At that time, the fens were a treacherous expanse of reed, water and winding causeways. It would be a dangerous journey. Sir Ralph had heard that nobody knew the lie of the land better than the landlord of the Fleece Inn in Southery. His name was Mucky Porter.

So, on the night of 30 April, Mucky Porter was lying fast asleep in bed, his wife snoring beside him, when something disturbed his slumbers. Someone was throwing stones at the bedroom window. He climbed out of bed and looked down into the street. Two of Sir Ralph's retainers were looking up at him: 'Are you Mucky Porter?'

'That's what they call me.'

'Are you on the side of Old Nol?'

'Well, why should I be? He's taken all my best customers to fight for him.'

'Would you be prepared to help the King?'

'I'll help anyone … if there's a few shillings involved.'

'Come with us, then.'

Mucky Porter pulled on his clothes, went to the stable, saddled a pony, and followed the two men to Snowre Hall. When he arrived, Sir Ralph Skipwith led him into the oak-panelled parlour and introduced him to the King. Mucky bowed.

'You are to lead the King over the ferry and across the fen to the Bell Tavern in Huntingdon.'

'Alright then,' said Mucky, and he bowed again.

He was asked to kiss the King's sword as proof of his loyalty. But still Sir Ralph's wife was uneasy. She looked this old fen slodger up and down and shook her head. She tugged her husband's sleeve and whispered into his ear: 'Surely it's not safe for one old man to lead the King of England across the Fen.'

Mucky had sharp ears and overheard her. He reached into his pocket and pulled out a grey goose feather. He pulled his knife from his belt and set to splitting the stem of the feather. As he did so he said: 'As long as fish have scales and birds have feathers, I will help you, and so will everybody else who belongs to the Brotherhood of the Grey Goose Feather.'

He handed the feather to the King.

'Now the whole Fen's on your side.'

Charles took the feather. Sir Ralph and his wife looked at one another and nodded … and it was agreed.

That night the King took off his wig and all his fine clothes. He put an old otter-skin cap on his head; he pulled on a dirty jacket and moleskin breeches. He fastened eel-skin gaiters about his shins and laced up a pair of muddy, tackety boots. He disguised himself as a fen-man.

The next morning Sir Ralph went to his stables and chose a pair of beautiful horses to carry the travellers safely to Huntingdon, each with a long and distinguished pedigree, each stamping and steaming and champing at the bit, each with a coat as sleek as a horse chestnut fresh from the shell.

The King climbed onto one, old Mucky climbed onto the other – he'd never ridden such a beauty – and they set off together. But they hadn't journeyed far when Mucky became aware that people were looking at them with surprise and suspicion: two old slodgers riding a pair of magnificent horses. He led the King to the Fleece Inn at Southery.

'Hold you hard.'

He helped the King down from the saddle and sat him in the snug with a flagon of ale. Then he led the two horses to the stable. He unbridled and unsaddled them. He gave each of them a blanket and a nosebag full of oats. In their place he brought out a couple of spavin-kneed ponies. The King climbed onto one, he climbed onto the other, and from that moment onwards nobody looked at them twice.

They rode side by side to the ferry over the River Ouse. It was controlled by Roundheads, Cromwell's men.

'Who goes there?'

Mucky Porter reached into his pocket and pulled out a split grey goose feather. Charlie Wag did the same.

'All right then! Quick … over the river!'

The Roundheads were fen-men and they understood. They asked no questions. Charles and Mucky led the ponies onto the ferry and they were taken across to the far side. They journeyed onwards, following the causeways and the higher ground until they reached Huntingdon. At the Bell Tavern they parted, but as Mucky Porter was turning to ride home the King said: 'Wait!'

He reached into his pocket and pulled out a purse. He dropped it into Mucky's hand.

'I thank you with all of my heart.'

The King lowered his head and ducked into the tavern. As soon as he was gone, Mucky opened the purse and looked inside. It was full of golden sovereigns. He chuckled to himself: 'That was a decent wage for a day's work. A purse full of money and two handsome nags nicely stabled at the Fleece.'

He set off for home with the King's pony following behind.

But in the days that followed, the news reached Cromwell's ears that the King had been allowed to cross the river. He was apoplectic with rage – and Cromwell was famous for his rages. He ordered the men who had been guarding the ferry to be brought before him. He told them that they would both be hanged in chains if they couldn't explain themselves. So the two men, with heads bowed, told their story, and when they'd finished Cromwell sighed: 'Well, it is better for a fen-man to let the King across the river, than it is for a fen-man to betray anybody who belongs to the Brotherhood of the Grey Goose Feather.'

And he set them free. Cromwell was a fen-man himself and he understood.

But poor Charlie Wag wasn't destined to reach Oxford. At Newark he was captured by the Presbyterian Scots. He surrendered to them. They promptly handed him over to Parliament and went home to Edinburgh £100,000 the richer.

The King was brought to trial and sentenced to death 'as a tyrant, traitor, murderer and public enemy to the good people of this nation'.

On the evening before the execution, 19 January 1649, Cromwell and his advisers were sitting in the banqueting hall in Whitehall, talking and making plans. Suddenly the door burst open. In came a breathless messenger from the King. He bowed to Cromwell: 'The King is too proud to beg for mercy, but he asks you to give him the help that you would give to anybody who carries this token.'

Onto the table in front of Cromwell, he dropped a split grey goose feather. He bowed again, turned and left the room.

Cromwell paled. He stared at the feather. He told his advisers to leave the room. All night he sat and wrestled with his conscience. The next morning, when servants came to clear the table, he was still sitting there, with great bags under his eyes. But in the end he decided to go ahead with the execution. On 30 January, dressed in a nightcap and cloak, Charles lost his head.

But it was said that Cromwell was never the same man again. He brooded, and his health broke. All the fen-men who had fought for him threw twisted goose feathers at his feet and returned to the fens. They wouldn't lift a pikestaff or a musket for him ever again.

In the Fleece Inn in Southery, old Mucky Porter heard about the death of Charlie Wag and he shed a tear into his flagon of ale. Years later he heard about the death of Old Nol, but this time his eyes were dry.

Fifteen long years passed. And then one summer's morning Mucky Porter, by now a very old man, was sitting outside the Fleece Inn soaking up the sunshine. He heard the clattering of hooves along the village street. He turned and saw two gentlemen dressed in fine clothes; they had curling wigs and pointed beards. He guessed they were heading to Newmarket for the horse racing. One of them reined in his horse and looked at the old man: 'Tell me, are you Mucky Porter?'

'That's what they call me.'

The gentleman turned to his companion.

'You know, many times I've heard the story of how this old man led my father across the fens all those years ago.'

Mucky Porter pulled himself up to his feet and bowed as best he could with his stiff joints. Straightaway he knew that this was the new King, Charles II.

The King smiled.

'Fetch a horse and come with me.'

The old man hobbled to the stable and came out a few minutes later riding a beautiful chestnut mare, the offspring of the original two. Charles, who had an eye for a good horse, was amazed.

'Come with me.'

They rode out of the village to Methwold Fen. At that time the draining of the fens had just begun, and that part of the fen was no longer a landscape of mire and reed, but had become an open stretch of rich, black fertile soil. The King, who had a share in the draining, led Mucky to the middle of it.

'I'd like to give you some of this new land, for yourself and your sons and your grandsons … and your family from this day onwards. How much do you want?'

Mucky Porter narrowed his eyes and scanned the fen with a shrewd fen-man's gaze. He lifted his arm and pointed: 'I'll have from that stump over to the west, along the length of the dyke to that mound ...' he swung his arm, 'and over to that old leaning oak over there. How many acres do you reckon I've got?'

The King raised an eyebrow.

'I would say you've got several acres there.'

And so it came about, that from that day to this, that part of the fen has been called the 'Methwold Severals'. And until a generation or so ago, it was farmed by Porters. And what's more, as any old fen-man will tell you: 'There was always something about the Porters' horses. They was always a cut above the average.'

26

LITTLE SAINT WILLIAM
OF NORWICH

When the excavations were being dug for the Chapelfield Shopping Centre in 2004, one of the backhoe operators reported what appeared to be a human skull lodged in a hole, 16ft underground. On investigation it proved to be the bottom of a well containing seventeen skeletons. Five of the skeletons had retrievable, testable DNA which indicated that they were Jewish.

This gruesome discovery marks the final chapter in a shameful episode in Norwich's history. And it marks the end of a story that began on 25 March 1144, when the body of a tanner's apprentice was found in a sack in Thorpe Wood. It was identified as being William, son of Wenstan, and it showed signs of a violent death. Within days rumours began to spread that the boy had died at the hands of the local Jews.

At that time there was a thriving Jewish community in Norwich. There were wine merchants, cheese and fishmongers, butchers and physicians, and a few extremely wealthy moneylenders. Supreme among the moneylenders was the Jurnet family. They were bankers and merchants who lent money to the Crown, the Church and to the rich and poor of Norwich. Their house, now called Wensum Lodge, still stands to this day by the river in King Street.

Isaac Jurnet was one of the wealthiest and most powerful Jews in England. But success and prosperity breeds resentment, and the payment of interest on a loan was as unpopular then as it is today. And after all, the citizens of Norwich reasoned, the Jews were infidels; they were not Christians. Indeed, they were implicated in the very death of Jesus Christ.

Sometimes it is convenient for a prejudice to become a story. Neither Church nor Crown saw any reason to refute or deny the rumour that was taking root in the imaginations of the populace of Norwich. Indeed, the heavily indebted church encouraged it.

The poisonous rumour was the unfounded suspicion that the Jews used the blood of children to make matzos (unleavened bread) for the feast of Passover. It wrapped itself around the unexplained death of William. It was whispered that the wealthy Jews of Norwich, who wore cloaks of leather and fur, had invited the skinner's apprentice to one of their homes on 20 March. They treated him kindly at first, and invited him to stay the night. But on the morning of the 21st – the feast of Passover – the chiefs among the Jews seized the boy as he was having his dinner, lacerated his head with thorns, crucified him and pierced his side to collect his blood. It was alleged that the Jews then put the body into a sack and took it into the woods to bury it, but they were surprised by the appearance of a forester and fled, leaving the sack hanging from the branch of a tree.

Witnesses were soon found. A monk called Theobald who had been converted from Judaism to Christianity and was now resident in the Norwich Priory told how in the ancient scriptures of his fathers it was written that every year a Christian must be sacrificed in some part of the world in contempt of Christ, whose death had been the cause of Jewish exile. Theobald told how lots had been drawn in that year, 1144, and Norwich had been chosen as the place of sacrifice. All the synagogues of England had given their assent.

A one-eyed Christian woman who worked as a servant in a Jewish household claimed to have seen the boy crucified in a room in her master's house, and said that she had delivered boiling water to scald the body.

Monks who examined the body testified that it had been scourged, and that the head bore the marks of a crown of thorns.

The case was brought to trial but, even by the standards of the time, the evidence was considered too insubstantial for a prosecution. But a story can be more damaging than a lawsuit. The body of William was buried first in Thorpe Wood. Then, by popular demand, it was moved to the cathedral grounds. It became a place of pilgrimage, and miracles were attributed to it. It was exhumed to be reburied in the chapter house. The monks claimed that when the body was lifted out of the ground it was uncorrupted, a sure sign that they had a saint on their hands. The shrine of a saint was a source of wealth to many holy houses. So the body was moved again, this time into the cathedral itself. The remains of St William's chapel can still be seen under the organ loft. It was said to be the place of many miracles.

The veneration of the shrine, and the accounts of miraculous happenings in the cathedral, ensured that the bitter story was told again and again, and with each telling an unfounded rumour hardened to fact. Hatred seethed and fermented – encouraged by those who owed money – towards the Jewish population of the city.

In 1172 the story became official truth when Thomas of Monmouth, a monk in the Benedictine Priory, wrote a history, called the *Life and Miracles of St William of Norwich*. But it would take another eighteen years for the legend to have its full effect.

In February 1190, there was a popular uprising against the Jewish quarter. All Jews found in their own houses were butchered, and those that had escaped to Norwich Castle are alleged to have committed mass suicide. With the massacre, of course, ledger books were destroyed and old debts disappeared from memory. Among the dead were seventeen corpses, flung head-first into a well at Chapelfield. Eleven of them were children.

This is the first recorded example of a 'blood libel' accusation being levelled against a Jewish community. It marked the beginning of a lamentably long list of similar slanders that have been the cause of massacres and injustices throughout Europe. Indeed, it was to protect the Jews of Prague from reprisals following similar accusations in the sixteenth century that Rabbi Judah Loewben Bezazel created the Golem. It was a man-made creature, almost human, of tremendous strength. If only there had been a Golem of Norwich too.

27

Six Norfolk Ghosts

The Groaning Well

When the pump on Whimpwell Street in Happisburgh went out of use, the villagers were reluctant to have it removed. They were worried that the well below it would start to groan again ... as it had done for years before the pump was installed, especially when a storm was brewing.

The groaning had first been heard more than 200 years before; and with it, a curious apparition had been witnessed by several men coming home late at night. They had seen a man making his way from Cart Gap towards the village. His head was hanging backwards and upside down between his shoulders as though it had been severed from his body and was held only by a flap of skin at the nape of his neck. His eyes rolled in their sockets. His severed windpipe wheezed and groaned. He wore a sailor's canvas clothes, but his feet were bare. A long, tarred pig-tail hung from his head and swung against the backs of his knees. In his arms he carried a sack.

One night two men followed the ghost. It led them to the well on Whimpwell Street. It leaned forwards and dropped its sack into the well, then vanished.

The next day, one of the men volunteered to be lowered down into the well by a rope. It was fastened around his waist, and in one hand he held a lantern. Six men fed the rope through their fingers. When he came to the water he shouted up: 'Fasten the rope!'

He reached under the surface with one arm. He felt something like a piece of slimy rope. He pulled. It was a pigtail. Soon a decomposing head appeared, still attached to its body by the skin on the nape of its neck.

The body was hauled out of the well, and then a sack was found in the water. Inside it was a pair of seaman's boots. The body was buried with its boots in an unmarked grave in Happisburgh churchyard. And from that day onwards, the ghost was never seen again. The people of Happisburgh searched Cart Gap and found a broken brandy keg hidden beneath a tangle of brambles. They assumed he'd been murdered in a smugglers' dispute.

But even though the ghost had vanished, the well was not silent. From its depths came a wheezing and groaning that didn't cease until the iron pump was set in place over it.

Abbot for Life

Alongside the River Bure to the south of Ludham are the ruins of St Benet's Abbey. It has a windmill built into what was once its gatehouse. It's more easily approached by water than by land. But anyone mooring close to the abbey for the night is likely to have his sleep disturbed by the sound of sudden, shrill screaming.

The abbey was founded by King Canute in about 1020. By the time of the Norman invasion in 1066 it was already established, and because of its remote position, had been constructed like a fortress. The abbey became one of the last outposts of the Saxon resistance. The Normans laid siege to it, but the monks held out for months. They had fish from the Bure and a limitless source of water. Nothing would bring the abbey to heel.

But there was one monk, a lowly brother who was good for little but trimming candles and sweeping floors. One of his offices was to check at dusk that the oak and iron doors of the gatehouse were firmly bolted against the invaders. Even though he could neither read nor write, he had a secret dream that one day he would become abbot. One evening, as he was casting his eyes over the great doors, a tantalising idea slipped into his mind. He pulled back the bolts and slipped through. He hurried towards the fires of the Norman encampment. The sentries seized him and dragged him to their commanders. They looked the monk up and down.

'What do you want?'

He looked at the ground.

'I could help you.'

'How?'

'If you paid me proper, I could leave the doors unbolted.'

One of the commanders lifted a purse from his belt. He opened it, and tipped a pile of golden coins onto his palm.

'How much?'

'No money … no money at all.'

'What then?'

'When the abbey has fallen you must make me abbot … abbot for life.'

The commanders looked at one another. Some unspoken understanding passed between them.

'Very well.'

The monk held out the wooden cross that hung about his neck.

'Do you swear on the holy rood?'

Each commander in turn clasped it.

'I swear you will be made abbot for life.'

The monk turned: 'Tomorrow night ... the doors will be unfastened.'

He hurried back to the abbey and locked the doors behind himself.

The next night the Normans entered the abbey. The monks were surprised in their dormitories. They were seized and bound, but no blood was shed. In the morning, they found themselves being herded into the church. They sat in their accustomed places, with their wrists bound behind their backs. Then they watched in astonishment as their abbot was stripped of his vestments before the high altar. A Norman priest summoned from the back of the church the little, lumpen dimwit who trimmed the candles. The monks saw that he alone was unbound. The vestments were ritually laid upon him. With all proper ceremony he was made abbot. The monks had no choice but to watch the investiture of their traitor brother. They watched as he led the procession down the aisle from the altar to the west door.

But as soon as the new abbot left the church, puffed up with pious triumph, his secret dream fulfilled ... his luck took a turn. He was roughly seized by Norman footsoldiers and dragged to the bell tower. A noose was hanging from the lowest window. He screamed and struggled to break free, but there was to be no mercy. The noose was looped around his neck and he was hanged in his robes of high office, his kicking feet just a few inches from the ground. The Normans had kept their word. He had been made abbot for life.

And even to this day, the shrill screams of the traitor monk are said to shatter the stillness of the night in the ruins of St Benet's Abbey on the banks of the River Bure.

∞

THE HEADLESS ROCKING HORSE

For many years, the Nun's Bridges in Thetford were troubled by a strange, troublesome spectre. Many sightings were reported of a seven year old boy whipping a headless wooden rocking horse to a galloping frenzy.

After the Dissolution of the Monasteries, the Benedictine Nunnery in Thetford was acquired by Sir Richard Fulmerston. He had it converted into a house. In 1569 his little nephew George, Lord Dacre came to live with him. George, who was heir to large tracts of land in Cumberland, had been orphaned. Sir Richard was his closest relative.

There was nothing little Lord George loved better than to climb onto the back of his painted rocking horse and set it rocking with such impetuous abandon that it lifted onto the fronts and backs of its rockers, almost throwing the boy to the floor. He would shout and strike the horse's dappled flank with a little leather whip.

Sir Richard watched him and thought about Cumberland.

On the night of 17 May, he pulled out the pin that joined the horse's front hooves to the rocker. The next morning Lord George Dacre tumbled from his horse at the height of his play. His head struck the wall and his brains were dashed out. The stain on the wall was still visible 200 years later.

But the little boy's spirit wouldn't rest. Time and again he troubled people on the Nun's Bridges, shouting and whipping his headless wooden horse to a frenzy of rocking. In the end, the people of Thetford decided that it was time to lay the ghost. A pound of new candles was carried to the bridge. They were blessed and then thrown into the Little Ouse.

'Little Lord George,' the vicar of Thetford shouted, 'do not return until these candles have been burned completely up!'

The ghost has not been seen since.

As for Sir Richard, his ghost was condemned to drive a spectral team of horses through the walled-up gateway of the old nunnery on the anniversary of his death. Although he and his team have no substance, they are said to loosen the bricks as they drive through, so that the wall has to be constantly repaired to this day.

THE SHRIEKING PITS

Between Aylmerton and West Runton, in the area known as Roman Camp, there are a number of circular depressions in the ground, some of them 20ft in diameter. They are part of a late Saxon iron industry. The iron was extracted from glacial sands here, and made into ingots in smelting furnaces. The pits are also associated with the ghost of a woman. She is described as being deathly pale and wearing a white dress. She runs from pit to pit, wringing her hands and shrieking. She peers into one hole after another and never finds what she is seeking.

The story is a familiar one. A jealous husband (history doesn't tell us whether or not his jealousy was justified) murdered his wife and his child in a fit of rage. Her body was found hidden in one of the pits and she was given a Christian burial. But the body of the baby was never found. Her distraught ghost is compelled to search for it, night after night, until the end of time.

THE LANTERN MAN

Before the enclosure of Irstead in 1810, at Heard's Hole in Alderfen Broad between Irstead and Neatishead, a malevolent jack-o'-lantern was frequently encountered. Mrs Lubbock, a local wise-woman, described it as 'rising and falling and twistering about'. If a traveller was carrying a lantern the spirit would smash it to the ground. If any traveller mocked it, it would follow him home and 'torch up at the windows' or knock him from his horse.

The spirit was said to be the ghost of a man called Heard. He had been guilty of some terrible, unspecified crime. The people of Irstead had, at some remote time, taken the law into their own hands and drowned him. The place of the drowning had been called 'Heard's Hole' ever since. And since then, Heard had haunted the area as a jack-o'-lantern or will-o'-the-wisp, especially on misty, roky nights.

The ghost always appeared at places Heard was said to have frequented when he was alive, following the same route night after night. It was so troublesome that the people of Irstead and Neatishead decided to lay it. Three men waited for it one roky night with bibles in their hands. As it approached they read verses at it, but the ghost knew its scripture. Whatever they read, it could speak the verse that followed in a voice so harsh and cold that it silenced them. The next night the three men took a boy with them. He had a pigeon hidden under his coat. When the jack-o'-lantern approached, one of them spoke his verses. Before the ghost could answer, the boy opened up his coat. The pigeon battered its wings and flew into the night. The ghost was so distracted that it lost its verse. It was never seen again.

THE CANDLESTICK IN THE POND

In the parish of Shelfanger, a dried-up pond is all that has survived of Bumblers Farm. The foundations have melted back into the fields. One of the inhabitants of the farm is sometimes still seen though; a woman in a high-waisted dress and a cap of the kind that was fashionable in the early years of the nineteenth century. She moves from room to room in a house that is no longer there.

The woman's name was Mrs Freeman. One winter's evening in 1814, she was involved in a dispute over a piece of land. She became so hysterical that she seized her husband's razor and slashed open her throat. With blood pouring onto her dress and apron she took a brass candlestick, ran out of the farmhouse into the darkness and hurled herself into the pond. The pond was dragged and her body was found. But the candlestick was never retrieved. As a suicide, she was buried against the north wall of the churchyard.

Seventy years later, the farm came into the possession of the Porcher family. Along with the deeds was a handwritten note, warning that if a candlestick were to be found in the pond, it should not be touched. The Porchers paid it little mind. In 1885 Mr Porcher decided that the pond needed to be dredged. Several tons of mud was removed from it. The day after the dredging, strange things began to happen in the farmhouse. Objects in the parlour were thrown about by an unseen agent. Doors opened and slammed shut, as though of their own free will. And a woman was seen, in dress and mob-cap, walking from room to room.

Mr Porcher told his farmhands to sift through the mud. A few hours later, a stable boy came running to him. He was holding a brass candlestick. Mr Porcher took it and threw it into the middle of the pond. It sank down beneath the mud and duckweed.

From that moment, all the strange disturbances ceased. But the spirit had been made uneasy. She didn't return to her rest, but continued to wander through the house. The Porchers would glimpse her from time to time … and she made them uncomfortable.

They left the house and sold the land. The property fell into decay. Bricks and timbers were taken for other buildings elsewhere. A lumpy field and a dry pond are all that's left of Bumbler's Farm. And a ghost that moves from room to room, in a farmhouse that is no longer there.

28

Sir Thomas Browne and the Hollow Cane

In the Haymarket in Norwich, there is a bronze statue of Sir Thomas Browne contemplating a funerary urn. It stands not far from the site of the house where Browne lived, and almost in the shadow of the church of St Peter Mancroft, where he is buried.

Sir Thomas Browne was born in London in 1605, the son of a silk merchant. After studying at Oxford and several continental universities, he established himself as a physician in Norwich. It is for his writings that he is remembered. Born into the era when the reasoning of the early Enlightenment had not yet displaced the lingering superstitions of Medieval Christianity, his writing married the new scientific empiricism with a belief in angels, witches and the promise of paradise. He was a man of prodigious and arcane learning. His books are baroque in their twisting argument, his sentences sometimes lasting for several pages.

One of his two most famous treatises is *Hydriotaphia, Urn Burial, or a Brief Discourse of the Sepulchral Urns lately found in Norfolk*. This is a meditation on the nature of time, 'which antiquates antiquities, and hath an art to make dust of all things', triggered by some Bronze Age urns that had been found at Walsingham.

The other is *The Garden of Cyrus, or the Quincunciall Lozenge or Network Plantations of the Ancients, Artificially, Naturally, and Mystically Considered* in which he sees in the pattern of five – as in the five spots of a dice – a structure that underlies animate and inanimate nature.

Many years after he died in 1682, a catalogue was found amongst his papers. It was what he called his *Musaeum Clausum*. It listed his treasures, amassed over a lifetime, long since dispersed. It included a treatise by King Solomon on the shadows cast by our thoughts; a lost poem by Ovid, wrapped up in wax; a painting of a seascape of floating icebergs with bears, foxes, walruses and rare fowls sitting on them; a precious stone taken from a vulture's head; ostrich and hummingbird eggs; and salt from the Sargasso Sea (a cure for scurvy).

Amongst these wonders was one object that would have had a particular resonance, both with Browne's own family history and with the history of his adopted city of Norwich. It was a hollow bamboo cane, in which it was alleged two Persian friars in the sixth century had brought the first eggs of the silkworm from China into the western world.

It had been through the trading of silk that Browne's father had made his fortune, and it would be through the manufacture of silk that Norwich would – for a while – make hers. It was an industry that was just beginning to gain momentum in England during Browne's lifetime. King James I, 'the wisest fool in Christendom', had been obsessed with silk. When he travelled he always had with him a casket of silkworms, looked after by a specially appointed 'Groom of the Chamber'. By the time of James' death in 1625, he had overseen the planting of 100,000 mulberry trees in eastern England. It would take another hundred years for his dream of 'English silk' to be realised (partly because he had planted the wrong kind of mulberry).

Since the arrival of Flemish and Walloon weavers in the early 1500s, there had been a thriving cloth manufacturing industry in Norwich. But it was the Huguenot craftsmen that fled France in the early eighteenth century who brought with them the sophistication and expertise needed for the manufacturing and weaving of silk. Many of them settled in Norwich. Soon the existing industry had married the new industry, and within two generations the big Huguenot families (the Martineaus, Columbines, Le Fevres and Tillettes) were among the wealthiest and most powerful merchants and entrepreneurs in England. It was said that any traveller approaching Norwich on a dark winter's evening in the late eighteenth century would be struck by the glare which seemed to hang over the city from the windows of countless workshops bright with candlelight as the city weavers worked until late into the night.

The fruits of their labours can be seen in Strangers Hall – itself the home of exiled French silk weavers – where the pattern books of the eighteenth-century weavers are still kept. The names of the fabrics they wove are as mysterious and iridescent as the stuffs themselves: alepine, watered tabinet, sarsanet, lustring, satin, arrasene, callinanco and bombazine. In Thorpe Hamlet there was a plantation of 1,500 mulberry trees, housing 300,000 silkworms at any one time, each capable of producing, as it pupated, up to a mile of silken thread.

And then, with the new efficiency of the mill-driven looms of the Industrial Revolution, the loom weavers of Norfolk became obsolete. The local industry went into a steep decline.

Sir Thomas Browne, contemplating his hollow cane, could not have imagined that within 150 years the humble silk worm would have brought about the rise and decline of his adopted city. But as he wrote in a letter to a friend in 1656:

> He that hath taken the true Altitude of Things, and rightly calculated the degenerate state of this Age, is not like to envy those that shall live in the next, much less three or four hundred years hence, when no Man can comfortably imagine what Face this World will carry.

In 1840, Browne's lead coffin was accidentally damaged by workmen digging in the chancel of St Peter Mancroft. Out of curiosity it was opened, and his skull and a lock of his hair were removed. They became the possession of a parish councillor who eventually passed them on to the Norwich Hospital Museum where they were displayed under a bell jar for many years. Eventually they were returned to St Peter Mancroft, and in 1922 a second internment was performed with proper ceremony. The skull was registered as having been laid to rest aged 316 years.

Sir Thomas Browne, contemplating the urn in the Haymarket, could be contemplating his own ashes. In *Urn Burial* he asks: 'Who is to know the fate of his bones?' It's hard to believe he wouldn't have enjoyed the story of his own skull, whose brainpan wove such elaborately patterned verbal arrasenes and sarsenets.

He would, I think, also have enjoyed the American writer Willie Morris, who describes crossing Park Avenue in New York, reciting from Browne's *Urn Burial*:

> And since death must be the Lucina of life, and even Pagans could doubt, whether thus to live were to die; since our longest sun sets at right descensions, and makes but winter arches, and therefore it cannot be long before we lie down in darkness and have our light in ashes …
>
> At that instant I was almost clipped by a taxicab, and the driver stuck his head out and yelled, 'Aincha got eyes in that head, ya bum?'

29

JOHN SKELTON AND THE MILLER OF DISS

John Skelton was one of the leading scholars of his time. He was appointed tutor to Prince Henry (later to become Henry VIII). He was an ordained priest, a triple laureate with degrees in rhetoric from Oxford, Cambridge and Leuven Universities. He was a poet and translator. He was also a scallywag.

In 1504, as a result of some disgrace or other, he was retired from regular attendance at court and made Rector of Diss. His behaviour soon caused a scandal. He was secretly married to a woman who lived in his house. When the people of Diss complained to the bishop that their Rector had sired a baby by a concubine, Skelton is said to have held the naked infant aloft in the pulpit and claimed it was as good a baby as any of theirs. When the bishop summonsed him to his palace in Norwich, Skelton brought two capons to pacify him. When the bishop gave him a dressing down despite the gift, Skelton told him that the capons were called 'Alpha' and 'Omega', the first and the last gifts he would ever give him.

His poetry took various forms, most famously his own 'Skeltonic' lines, full of ragged, energetic alliteration. Here's an example, his account of Elynoare Rummynge, the landlady of a notorious inn:

Her lothely lere
Is nothynge clere,
But ugly of chere,
Droupy and drowsy,

Scurvy and lowsy;
Her face all bowsy,
Comely crynklyd,
Woundersly wrynkled,
Lyke a rost pygges eare,
Brystled wyth hair.
Her lewde lyppes twayne,
They slaver, men sayne,
Lyke a ropy rayne,
A gummy glayre:
She is ugly fayre;
Her nose somdele hooked,
And camously crooked,
Never stoppynge,
But ever droppynge …

After Skelton's death in 1529, a collection of stories about him was published – many of them apocryphal – called 'The Merie Tales of Skelton'. Here's one of them.

As Rector of Diss, Skelton was entitled to have his grain ground free of charge. His maidservants soon discovered that the flour that came back from the mill weighed considerably less than the grain that went. Mistress Skelton complained to her husband and John the Miller was sent for. When he was accused of stealing the grain the miller shook his head: 'Surely I never deceived you. If you can prove that I did, then do with me as you list.'

Skelton told one of his servants to carry his grain to the mill, to watch the grinding and to never take his eyes off it. But the miller was determined to steal his portion as before. He told his wife to throw one of their children into the millpond. Soon she was crying: 'Help! Help! My child is drowning!'

The servant ran outside, dived into the water and saved the child. When he came back to collect the flour the miller thanked him with tears in his eyes.

But when Skelton's maidservants came to the baking, the flour was as short as it had been before. Skelton sent for the miller.

'You have not used me well; once again I'm wanting in flour.'

'How could that be?' said the miller, 'you sent your man to watch me!'

'If you don't explain to me which way you've played the thief ... then I'll have you hanged.'

So the miller explained the trick he'd played. Skelton stroked his chin.

'I see,' he said, 'well, unless you can do what I tell you, it'll be the gallows for you.'

'What is that?'

'Unless you can steal the cup from my table while I'm sitting at meat, you shall not escape justice.'

That night the miller watched outside the window until Skelton was sitting at the table and his supper had been served. Then he set fire to one of his pigsties. Soon the alarm went up.

'Fire! Fire!'

Skelton ran outside to see what the matter was. John the Miller slipped through the door and stole his cup. When the fire had been put out, Skelton returned to his table. He called for a cup of ale. The maidservants curtsied: 'It has gone missing, sir.'

Skelton called for the miller. Soon he arrived with the cup in his hand.

'You are a notable knave,' he said, 'and you should be hanged ... and unless you can perform one more feat of cunning, you shall be!'

The miller dropped to his knees.

'What is it, sir?'

'Unless you can steal the sheets from my bed, while my wife and I are sleeping, it'll be the end of you.'

Now the miller's son, whose name was Jack, worked for Skelton. The miller gave Jack a tub of warm, yeasty water and told him to hide under Skelton's bed. When Skelton and his wife were snoring, Jack anointed the sheets with yeast. Skelton woke with a start. The bed was wet and foul smelling. He shook his wife's shoulder: 'What mistress, have you pissed the bed?'

'Nay sir, it is you that has done it.'

Soon there was a great strife between them. A maidservant was called to change the sheets. She threw the foul sheets under the bed, thinking that the next morning she would have them fetched away. Jack waited until Skelton and his wife were fast asleep. He took the sheets and carried them back to his father. When washing day came, the sheets were missing. Skelton called for the miller.

The miller arrived at the door with the sheets in his arms.

'How did you do it?'

The miller told his story.

'Now good master, forgive me, according to your promise.'

'No,' said Skelton, 'you must do yet one more feat, and it shall be this. You must steal my priest out of his bed at midnight, and take him he knows not where ... and if you fail you'll find no favour.'

The miller went out and collected a bucketful of snails. He bought some thin wax candles and fixed them to the snails' shells. Between the hours of eleven and twelve at night, he entered the church of St Mary. He lit the candles and let the snails crawl this way and that. He went into the vestry and found the rector's vestments. He put them on. Then he rang the church bell.

The priest was asleep in his little cell in the churchyard. Suddenly he was woken by the bell. He looked out of his window and saw light in the church. He ran across the churchyard. When he entered the church door, his eyes were met by a wonder. There were lights moving of their own accord across the church floor. In front of the high altar, a figure in full vestments was standing with a book in his hands. The priest called out: 'In the name of the Father, the Son and the Holy Ghost, what art thou that stands in this holy place?'

The miller lifted his head: 'I am St Peter, who keeps the keys to Heaven; you know that no one can enter Paradise unless I let him in. I have been sent to fetch you.'

'Me!'

'Because you have done good deeds and served God well, he has sent for you before doomsday comes, so that you shall not know the Trouble of the World.'

'O, blessed be God! I am ready. But first let me go and distribute such things as I have amongst the poor.'

'No! If you delight more in your own goods than in the joys of Paradise you are not for God. Prepare yourself, come with me now.'

The miller lifted a large, empty flour sack.

'Climb into this sack which I have brought for you. Soon you will be there.'

The priest climbed gratefully into the sack. The miller tied its neck with a good double knot. He put out the lights, and put everything back into its proper place. Then he slung the sack onto his back. When he came to the churchyard stile he flung the sack over the top. The priest cried: 'Aaargh!'

'These are the pangs you must abide before you come to Heaven.'

He lifted the sack onto his shoulder. The mill was on the other side of a hill. The miller climbed to the top, then dropped the sack again. It rolled down to the bottom.

'Ow! Ouch! Good St Peter, these are the sorest pangs that ever I had. Where am I now?'

'Give thanks unto God that you have patience to abide all this pain. For now you are going to ascend to Paradise.'

When the miller reached his house, he tied a rope to the sack, threw it over a bar in his chimney and hoisted the priest upwards.

The next morning the Sexton rang the bell for Mass. The people of Diss flocked to the church. But there was no sign of the priest. Word reached Skelton's ears that the priest had vanished. He went to the Miller's house.

'Where is my good priest?'

The miller pointed to the chimney. Skelton shouted: 'Where are you?'

The priest replied: 'Heaven, Hell or Limbo … I know not where!'

Skelton was amazed. He asked the miller to tell his tale. When the miller had finished, he said: 'God curse you … for putting holy ornaments upon your own knavish back, you shall hang!'

The miller dropped to his knees: 'Pardon me! I did only what you required of me.'

'That is not strictly true,' said Skelton, 'but if you can steal my horse from my stable, with two of my men watching over him, then I will truly pardon you. You have my very word on it. If, on the other hand, they catch sight of you, then they shall have my instruction to strike off your head … for it would be a better thing that such a scoundrel as you should die than live.'

The miller remembered that a thief had been hanged the day before. His body was still swinging from the gallows. That night he cut the thief down. With a long, sharp knife he cut off the thief's head. He sprinkled it with flour and put his own cap on its head. He fastened the head to the end of a pole and approached Skelton's stable. The door was ajar.

Inside, Skelton's men were waiting with sharpened swords at the ready. They saw the door move. Then a head appeared; the miller's head. It seemed to look from left to right. They crept to the doorway, raised their swords, and struck. The head rolled across the floor.

'We have him!'

They lifted the head and ran to Skelton's house.

'We have him! We have him!'

Skelton came running down the stairs. He seized the head and looked at it. He was looking into the face of the cutpurse who had been hanged the day before. Skelton ran across to the stable. His horse was gone.

'Fetch me the miller!'

John the miller came to Skelton's house.

'Where's my horse?'

'Safe enough, master.'

The miller told his story. Skelton considered and said: 'You are worthy to be hanged ten times over for you do excel all the thieves that I ever knew or heard of. But for my promise's sake I forgive you, on the condition that you become an honest man and leave behind all your craft and false-dealing. For such cleverness and cunning, if put to God's service, might outwit the Devil himself.'

John the miller gave his word, and Skelton gave him his blessing.

30

THE VISIONS OF
ST FURSEY

About 3 miles due west of Gorleston, you can see the ruins of Burgh
Castle. It is one of the 'Forts of the Saxon Shore' built in the late
third century by the Romans, as protection from the incursions of
Saxon pirates. Three sides of the fort's massive flint and brick walls
remain. It is now situated a long way inland, but when it was built,
it would have stood on the westernmost spit of a peninsula that
looked out across a huge tidal estuary, a remote position exposed
to the elements that wouldn't have been a favourite posting among
Roman soldiers.

After the Roman Empire crumbled in the late fifth century, a
dynasty of Saxon kings established themselves in East Anglia.
The first we know of is Wuffa, who reigned in the 570s. By the
end of that century, Christian missionaries were at work in the
area. King Raedwald, based in Rendlesham in Suffolk, was semi-
converted. He worshipped at two altars – one dedicated to the old

familiar deities: Odin, Thor, Freya and Balder … and the other to the new 'White Christ'.

While England was plunged into the chaos of the 'Dark Ages' between the end of the Roman occupation and the establishment of the new Saxon dynasties, Ireland maintained an unbroken monastic Christian tradition, alongside its ancient pagan culture. So it was from Ireland that many of the early Christian missionaries came. One of them was St Fursey. He was the son of a pagan father and a Christian mother. His great-uncle was St Brendan. As a boy he had been taken under Brendan's wing, and his sanctity had been revealed at an early age. In a vision he was instructed to become a 'more zealous labourer for the Lord'. And so, with two of his brothers, also monks, he set forth across the Irish Sea for England. The journey, in a currach, an elongated coracle made of cowhides stretched over a wooden frame, would have been a perilous one. They travelled over sea and land until they reached the court of Sigeberht, King of East Anglia.

Sigeberht was a Christian who had been converted by St Felix, and he welcomed the Irish monks. He offered them the ruins of the Roman fort at Burgh Castle as a place of sanctuary.

The Irish monastic tradition, like that of the desert fathers, was one of extreme asceticism. They liked to inhabit remote places, and their writings are filled with an ecstatic delight in the forces of nature and the beauties and consolations of the natural world. The ruined castle on its headland, exposed to the winds and overlooking the great expanse of the Yare estuary with its tides, muddy sands, gulls and seals would have been pleasing to Fursey and his brothers.

In the early 630s they built a church, an oratory, of wattle and daub surrounded by monastic cells inside the castle walls. Whatever the season, Fursey is described as wearing no more than a robe of thin cloth. From that simple monastery he began his ministry. Word of his sanctity spread; rumour had it that before he left Ireland he had raised the twin children of King Brendinns from the dead by virtue of his prayers. He travelled on foot, evangelising among the Saxon villages of East Anglia and making many conversions.

Two of Fursey's miracles during his sojourn at Burgh Castle are recorded. It is said that when the monastery was first completed, it lacked only a bell. As St Fursey was pondering the problem – and a bell was an expensive item in seventh century East Anglia – a local widow lost her only son. Keening with grief, she brought the body to the monastery so that the boy could be laid to rest by the Irish brothers. Fursey went out to meet the funeral procession as it made its way along the headland to the monastery. As he drew close, a bright light shone in the sky overhead. The grievers looked up and saw an angel descending from the heavens. It was carrying a silver bell in its hands. The angel gave the bell to Fursey and then winged its way back into the clouds. Fursey swung the bell, and as the clapper struck the metal, a note of astonishing sweetness filled the air. The dead boy, stretched out on his bier, suddenly lifted his head and looked about himself. He sat up and rubbed his eyes. He climbed down from the bier as though he had never been ill. He took his mother's hand. And the mourners turned, their hearts filled with happiness, and made their way home. The bell was hung in the sacristy, and years later the boy became a monk and joined the brothers at Burgh Castle.

On another occasion there was a time of terrible famine. All across the region harvests had failed. In the monastery the Irish brothers were starving. Fursey and a brother called Lactan went into a field beside the old castle walls. They began to till the ground with a spade and a rake. Fursey then scattered seed. He returned to the oratory and knelt in prayer. Within three days the barley had sprouted, grown both ear and beard, paled and ripened so that on the fourth day the brothers could go out with sickles and fill their granaries with grain and their stacks with barley straw.

But Fursey is most remembered for his visions. During one of them, he was carried up to a great height by angels. They told him to look back at the world. He saw a dark valley, and hanging above it in the air he saw four blazing fires. He asked the angels: 'What are the fires?'

'They are the fires that will consume the world. They are called Falsehood, Covetousness, Discord and Cruelty.'

The four fires drew together into one enormous conflagration. Fursey cried out: 'Masters – the fire is coming near me!'

But the angels replied: 'It will not burn you, because you did not kindle it.'

Then one of the angels divided the flames, and the other two flew on either side of Fursey to protect him from harm, and they led him down through the flames and back to where his body lay in the valley far below.

The Venerable Bede, in his *Ecclesiastical History of the English Peoples* wrote:

> An old brother of our monastery, who is still living, testifies that he once knew a truthful and devout man who had met Fursey in the province of the East Angles, and heard of these visions from his own mouth. He added that it was a frosty and bitter winter's day when Fursey told his story; and yet, though he wore only a thin garment, he was sweating profusely as though it had been summer, either because of the consolation or the terror of his recollections.

After ten years at Burgh Castle, there came a period of political turbulence, as heathen Mercian warriors fought their way into East Anglia. Fursey climbed aboard his currach one last time and journeyed to France. He died in Peronne, where his skull is still kept as a holy relic.

Perhaps the last word on Fursey should be given to Francis Palgrave, writing in the mid-nineteenth century:

> The stranger, on the dark marshy shores of the oozy Yare, contemplating the lichen-crusted ruins of the Roman castle … scarcely supposes that those grey walls once enclosed the cell of an obscure anchorite, destined … to exercise a mighty influence upon the … genius of Christendom. This was … Fursey, who, received in East Anglia by King Sigebert, there became enwrapped in the trances that disclosed to him the secrets of the world beyond the grave.

31

FIDDLERS AND TUNNELS

In 1933, Norfolk County Council workmen were widening the crossroads at Fiddler's Hill, halfway between Binham and Warham. In order to do so, they had to cut through the edge of a Bronze Age barrow. As they were digging, they unearthed a mixture of human and animal bones. They were of a much later date than the barrow, but still badly decayed, having been in the ground for several centuries. When they were pieced together, they were reckoned to be the skeletons of a human and a dog. There was great local interest and the *Norwich Mercury* ran an article on the discovery with the headline: 'Does Warham Discovery Prove Old Legend True?'

There is an old tradition that between St Mary's Priory at Binham and the Priory of Our Lady of Walsingham, there stretched a long underground passageway by which monks could travel in secret and move sacred relics from one holy house to another without fear. There was certainly a mysterious doorway in the church of Binham Priory, now the parish church, and several possible entrances at Walsingham … but no one dared explore the passage because of its ghost. A tall man, dressed in a dark Benedictine habit, was said to walk the tunnel. Sometimes he was seen above the tunnel, shaking his head and peering to left and right as though he was searching for something. Sometimes only his footsteps were heard, echoing behind the bricked up doorway in St Mary's church.

Then, one bright morning two centuries ago, a man appeared in Binham with a fiddle tucked under his arm. He played in the street with his hat on the pavement for farthings. He had a little terrier with a ragged ruff around its neck that would dance on its hind legs as he played. He played in public houses for mugs of ale. He brought news and gossip from Fakenham, Norwich and Kings Lynn. He sang songs and sold chapbooks and ballad sheets. He slept in barns and hedges, or any house that would offer him comfort.

He'd been in Binham for a week or so, gathering talk for his next port of call, when someone drew his attention to the old story of the passageway.

'Show me the entrance,' said the fiddler. In one version of the story, his name was Jimmy Griggs and his dog was called Trap.

He was taken to the blocked doorway in the church. He put his ear to the cold bricks.

'I don't hear nothing.'

That night, after several ales, he put a proposition to the men of Binham.

'I'll tell you what lads, I was thinking of heading Walsingham way. Why don't I take the old tunnel?'

The room went quiet. 'You'll have heard about the dark monk, Jimmy?'

The fiddler laughed. 'You Binham boys are afraid of your own shadders. I've slept in ruins, in church porches … and I've yet to see a ghost.'

'We'll have to ask the parson.'

'You ask whoever you please. I'll meet you at the church on Saturday morning, and I'll play my fiddle all the way to Walsingham. That way, you'll hear me and you can follow along up above and see which way the passage runs.'

The next morning a deputation of village men knocked at the parson's door. And the parson, being an antiquarian in a modest way, was enthusiastic about the scheme and paid the blacksmith to bring a hammer and a crowbar to the church and break open the old doorway.

When the fiddler and his dog arrived on Saturday morning, the whole village had filled the church. There were husbands and wives, children tugging at their mothers' arms, old village codgers leaning on sticks, housemaids giving apprentices the eye … the building was filled with an atmosphere of holiday high spirits. Seeing the crowd, Jimmy lifted his fiddle to his chin, flourished his bow and played 'Jockey to the Fair'. He danced up the aisle, with his dog jigging behind him.

He turned to the newly-opened doorway in the north wall. Beyond it, a damp cobbled floor disappeared downwards into utter darkness. A smell of old, mouldy air blew from it into the church. He was playing 'Bobbing Joan' as he ducked his head and stepped cautiously onto the slippery stones. He vanished from sight into the pitch-black shadow.

The crowd rushed outside.

'Shhh!'

From beneath the green turf of the churchyard they could hear the 'Red Petticoat Hornpipe'.

To their surprise the fiddler was heading north-west. The parson scratched his head. 'Could the passage have led to Hales Manor or Holkham?'

The crowd followed the sound through the village. From under the brick floor of the dairy at Westgate farm they caught clear strains of 'Speed the Plough'.

From under the sheep pasture at Short Lane Farm they heard 'Lovely Nancy'.

From beneath Haystack Lane came 'The Devil among the Tailors'.

At the crossroads it was 'England's Glory'.

The crowd climbed up onto the old green mound, chattering and laughing ... but suddenly the music seemed to have stopped.

'Shhhh, can you hear anything?'

They lay down with their ears to the turf ... but there was no sound.

'Maybe he's turned a corner.'

They scattered in all directions and listened; then they regrouped, shaking their heads.

'Nothing, not a murmur.'

All day they listened. Some men rode to Walsingham to see whether the fiddler had arrived, and was playing behind some ancient doorway in the priory ruin ... but all to no avail. He had vanished, and was never seen again, though in some versions of the story his little dog Trap appeared through the doorway in Binham church several days later, with his tail curled up between his legs, shivering and shaking at some terror he had no words to describe.

And from that day to this, that green hill at the crossroads between Binham and Warham, that ring-barrow has been called Fiddlers Hill.

A similar tale is told in Kings Lynn. According to local legend, Isabella, the wife of Edward II, described as the most beautiful woman in Europe, was imprisoned in Castle Rising. She had been living a dangerous life. Tiring of Edward's weak rule and his dalliances with various handsome courtiers, she had taken Roger Mortimer as a lover, overthrown her husband and assumed the mantle of monarch until her son came of age. It has been hinted that she and Mortimer were also implicit in Edward's murder.

Her son, however, was his mother's child. At the age of thirteen he overthrew Mortimer and Isabella, and prematurely took the crown for himself. Mortimer was executed, but his mother, whom he loved, was placed under house arrest. She lived out the rest of her life at Castle Rising, as Dowager Queen.

By now Isabella was known as 'the she-wolf of France' for the bloody revenge she had taken upon Edward ll's baronial supporters – one of them had been fed to the dogs. But at Castle Rising, she was given all the trappings of her status. She had jesters and musicians, ladies-in-waiting, and knights and squires to serve her. Lavish banquets were held in her honour. The only condition of her imprisonment was that she should not show her face in public.

It was for this reason that she had an underground passage built from Castle Rising to the Red Mount Chapel in Kings Lynn – a 10-mile stretch. It enabled her to worship at the chapel without breaking Edward III's decree.

After Isabella's death, the castle and the tunnel were said to be haunted by a beautiful, snow-white she-wolf with fiery eyes and fangs that dripped blood. Small wonder then, that the good burghers of Kings Lynn gave the ancient passageway a wide berth. It became more folk-memory than fact … until one day a drunken fiddler called Curtis, with his dog at his heels, turned up in Kings Lynn. He heard the old tale and made the same boast as his fellow journeyman in Binham. A crowd above followed the music over the Gaywood River, through South Wootton … and then, somewhere on Ling Common, there was a sudden silence. Neither fiddler nor dog was seen again … although it's said that on still nights the music of a fiddle can still be heard on the common, though what tune it's playing, no one knows.

32

THE SANDRINGHAM PALS

War memorials across the country bear testament to the many soldiers and civilians whose lives were lost in the two World Wars of the twentieth century. The inscription on Sandringham's war memorial, carved in crumbled gothic script, is unusually long. Many of the soldiers listed on the memorial died on the same day – 12 August 1915.

The E Company of the 5th Territorial Battalion of the Royal Norfolk Regiment known as 'The Holy Boys', all came from the same place. They were all staff of the Royal Estate at Sandringham. They had been formed at the request of their employer, King Edward VII. They were one of many groups of 'Pals', men who were familiar to one another, who enlisted together in the autumn of 1914. In this case, they fell easily into ranks – Frank Beck, the land agent of the estate, and his two nephews became officers. Butlers, head gamekeepers, head gardeners and foremen became NCO's, while labourers, grooms and servants became Privates.

After a period of training, they set sail from Liverpool on 30 July 1915. They arrived at Suvla Bay, Gallipoli, on the 10th of August. Already the fighting was intense. They were ordered inland to dig trenches in the blistering heat; each man was given a ration of two pints of water to last him three days.

The Turkish army was well armed, and the trees were full of snipers, with their faces painted green. They were impossible to see.

At four o' clock on the afternoon of 12 August, the Norfolk Regiment was given the order to attack. Colonel Horace Proctor-

Beauchamp waved his cane and shouted: 'On, the Norfolks, on!'
Captain Frank Beck and the Sandringham Pals fixed their bayonets
and advanced at the double. They entered an area of woodland
under fierce shelling and rifle fire ... and vanished. They were
never seen again. Their bodies were never found. Not one of them
was taken as a prisoner of war.

General Sir Ian Hamilton, the British Commander-in-Chief at
Gallipoli reported:

> There happened a most mysterious thing ... the fighting grew
> hotter ... Colonel Beauchamp still kept pushing on, driving the
> enemy before him ... Among these ardent souls was ... a fine
> company enlisted from the King's Sandringham Estates. Nothing
> more was ever seen or heard of any of them. They charged into the
> forest and were lost to sight and sound.

Four years after the war, a golden fob watch turned up in Istanbul.
It had belonged to Frank Beck and was returned to England
and presented to his daughter on her wedding day. A number of
unidentifiable skeletons were discovered in the area of the wood
with the shoulder flashes of the 5th Norfolks. But hundreds of the
'Holy Boys' died at Gallipoli. The mystery remained unsolved.

Then, on the fiftieth anniversary of the Gallipoli Landings in
1965, a former New Zealand sapper who had fought that day
came forward with an extraordinary story. Frederick Reichardt
and three fellow veterans swore that on the afternoon of 12 August
1915 they had seen a great wonder. They had watched a formation
of six or eight loaf-shaped clouds hovering over the wood where
the Norfolk Regiment was fighting. One of the clouds had lowered
itself and settled on the wood. The New Zealanders had seen the
Sandringham Pals running into the cloud, their bayonets fixed.
Then, before their eyes, the cloud had slowly risen and rejoined
the other clouds that were hovering overhead. They had silently
drifted away, leaving no trace of Captain Beck and his men. The
disappearance was a clear case of alien abduction. The vanishing of
the E Company became a UFO story.

In total 36,000 Commonwealth servicemen died in the Dardanelles. Of these, 13,000 lie in unidentified graves, their tombstones bearing the epitaph: 'A soldier, known unto God'. A further 14,000 were never found at all.

With the story of the Sandringham Pals we are left with two possible endings: In one they lie with thousands of others, caught between sniper fire, machine gun bullets and exploding shells, dead and uncounted in Turkish soil. In the other story, they are in some other dimension. They are still dressed in their khaki. They are sitting facing each other in two rows, their rifles between their knees. Captain Frank Beck is counting heads: 'Well, we're all here, lads, present and correct.'

'What happened, Sir? One minute we're dodging Johnny Turk and the next ...'

'Thass a rum'n, this fret come down and the next thing you know ...'

'It's a rum'n indeed!'

'Anyone got a smoke?'

'There you go, Billy.'

'Could be a hell of a site worse I reckon.'

'Any idea what time it is, Sir?'

Frank Beck unbuttons his jacket and reaches inside: 'Damn it, my watch must have dropped clean out of my pocket, somewhere between the trench and ... wherever the dickens we are now.'

33

SIR BERNEY BROGRAVE

Above the north door of Worstead Church there are the hatchments (coat of arms) of Sir Berney Brograve and his two wives.

Sir Berney inherited the manors of Worstead, Waxham and Horsey from his father in the mid-eighteenth century. When he came to his inheritance, he was already a notorious hedonist and wild man who had scattered his 'portrait' (his bastards) over the countryside.

The family crest includes a red hand – it can be seen in the top left corner, above three lions – because, it is said, one of his ancestors had whipped a boy to death. Certainly his father had killed a Norfolk gentleman, Henry Branthwayt, in a duel in London. He had kissed his victim and ridden away. The family was notorious, but it was Berney who would set the seal on its reputation.

He lived in Waxham Hall, farmed his own land and had 100 workmen lodging in his house. They all dined in the great hall together, and Sir Berney 'every now and then knocked down a bullock for them to live upon'.

William Marshall, the author of *The Rural Economy of Norfolk*, paid him a visit and described him:

> His person is gross, his appearance Bacchanalian – his dress that of a slovenly gentleman. There is a politeness in his manner: and his conversation bespeaks a sensible intelligent mind: borne away, however, by a wildness and ferocity which is obvious in his countenance and discovers itself in every word and action.

Sir Berney's fights, wagers and debts went into local legend. When a chimney sweep had worked his way through the main chimneys of Waxham Hall, he charged Sir Berney what seemed a fair fee. Sir Berney thought the charge too high and challenged him to a fight. If the sweep won he would get his money; if he lost, he would get nothing but a good thrashing. The sweep agreed. Sir Berney threw off his jacket, rolled up his sleeves, lifted his fat fists and began to give the sweep a drubbing. But the sweep had been shrewd enough to keep his work clothes on. With every punch, a black cloud of soot rose into the air, filling Sir Berney's eyes and nose and throat ... and as he coughed and choked, the sweep floored him with an upper-cut to the chin. Sir Berney crawled to the ottoman where his jacket lay, pulled out a purse and paid him. It's said that it took a week of hard drinking for him to wash the taste of soot from his throat.

In those days, Waxham Hall was haunted by six of Sir Berney's ancestors who had all died violent deaths on the field of battle. There was Sir Ralph who was killed by Saracens in the Crusades; Sir Edmund who died in the Baron's Wars; Sir John who had perished from a festering wound at Agincourt; Sir Francis who had been killed at Bosworth Field; Sir Thomas who had been felled by a musket at Marston Moor; and Sir Charles who had met his end at Ramillies. One New Year's Eve, Sir Berney took the notion to invite them all to supper. He ordered his servants to prepare seven places at the dining table, with candles burning, wine glasses filled, and roasted meat to each platter. When the food had been served, he sat at the table and told his servants to close and lock the doors. They did as they were told. Listening at the doors, they heard a great chinking and clinking of glasses, an uproar of toasting, a clattering of knives against pewter. As the clock struck midnight, the noise suddenly ceased. They opened the doors and found the remnants of a feast, with bones and spilt wine and chairs tipped backwards. The room was cold and empty but Sir Berney was at his place still, his cheeks flushed pinker than ever with wine and port ... and his hair had turned as white as snow.

Sir Berney kept a pack of ferocious hunting dogs. Everyone in the neighbourhood knew to keep indoors when Sir Berney was hunting. The kennel keeper was a local man, as tough as old boots, but even he was a little wary of his charges. One time, the keeper was passing through Hempstead, and stopped at the Royal Sovereign Inn. The landlord had a reputation as a star-reader and fortune-teller. The keeper, over a pint or two, consulted him. At first the landlord was reluctant to speak; he shook his head and kept silent. But the keeper gave him no peace and pressed a florin into his hand for his prediction. The landlord looked at the keeper with a sorry gaze: 'You will meet with a violent end, and your body will not be buried.'

A few days later as the keeper was cleaning the kennels at Waxham Hall, Sir Berney's dogs turned on him, tore him limb from limb and ate him, leaving only the brass buttons of his breeches scattered across the kennel floor. And did the savagery of his dogs cure Sir Berney of his passion for hunting? Not a bit of it. It was said that he loved his pack the more for it.

On another occasion, Sir Berney rode out to Worstead where his men were harvesting black beans. He sat and watched them for a while, then leapt down from his horse's back, seized the scythe from the hands of one of them and set to work himself. He cut the stalks down faster than any of his men. After ten minutes he stopped, wiped the sweat from his forehead with the sleeve of his jacket and bellowed, 'Damn the lot of you, I could out-mow the Devil!'

'You could, could you?'

Sir Berney and his men turned towards the voice. Standing under an ash tree at the edge of the field was a man they'd never seen before. He was tall, pale and thin, dressed as a farmer with a jacket and breeches of black linen. But where his boots should have been there were polished hooves, and jutting through the top of his tri-corn hat were two horns.

'Meet me here tomorrow at first light. Stake out 2 acres, one for me and one for you. If you can out-mow me, then you're as good as your word. If not – then your soul is mine.'

There was a flash. Sir Berney and his men covered their eyes with their hands. When they looked again, the Devil was gone.

So everything was made ready. Two acres of black beans were staked out. Two scythes were sharpened. A whetstone was set beside each scythe. The word spread that Sir Berney had finally met his match.

But that night sir Berney went to the forge of the Worstead blacksmith.

'I want a hundred rods of hard black iron, each one the height of a beanstalk.'

The blacksmith worked all night, and in the darkness before daybreak, Sir Berney took the rods and planted them among the beans in the Devil's acre.

At first light the Devil appeared and seized a scythe. Sir Berney took the other and they set to work, each at his own acre. But the iron rods took their toll. Again and again the Devil had to stop to sharpen his scythe. When Sir Berney had cut a half of his acre, Old Nick had barely cut a quarter. He threw down his scythe, mopped his forehead with a crimson handkerchief and shouted across: 'I say, Berney Bor, these bunks (weeds) do cut damned hard!'

There was a flash of light, a whiff of sulphur … and the Devil was gone.

But in the end, Sir Berney's drinking, gambling, feasting, hunting and general profligacy piled debt upon debt until he owed so much money that bankruptcy and limbo (debtor's prison) began to beckon. He summoned his Old Adversary, and sold his soul for the sum of his debts. The contract between Sir Berney and the Devil was written upon parchment. They spat on their palms, shook hands, and the Devil vanished, leaving a heap of coins that matched Sir Berney's debts to the farthing.

Another ten years of outrageous hedonism would pass before Sir Berney finally leaned his head against a pillow and breathed his last. Not many mourned his passing. In his last decade he had accumulated greater debts than ever before. After he died he called to the Devil: 'Here I am!'

But the Devil had been doing his homework. He came to Sir Berney and shook his head.

'I've been reading through your account, and it seems to me that if I take you with me, within a fortnight you'll be top dog and I'll be playing second fiddle ... so here's your contract back, and away with you!'

Well, there are two ends to the story. Some say that Sir Berney Brograve was condemned to linger in this world (neither hell nor heaven would have him), and his ghost can still be seen on certain nights of the year, riding the causeway between Waxham and Worstead.

And some say that Sir Berney said to the Devil: 'If you won't take me, then where shall I go?'

And the Devil, forgetting himself, replied: 'You can go to Hell!'

And Sir Berney took him at his word, and now there are two Devils in Hell ... though who plays first and who plays second fiddle is anybody's guess.

NORFOLK PLACE
NAMES INDEX

BIBLIOGRAPHY

Ashwin & Davison, *An Historical Atlas of Norfolk*, Phillimore

Barrett, W.H., & Garrod, R.P., *East Anglian Folklore*, R. & K. Paul

Barrett, W.H., *More Tales from the Fens*, R. & K. Paul

Barrett, W.H., *Tales from the Fens*, R. & K. Paul

Bede, *Ecclesiastical History of the English People*, Penguin

Blomefield, Revd Francis, *An Essay Towards a Topographical History of the County of Norfolk*, Gutenberg

Branston, Brian, *Gods of the North*, Thames & Hudson

Briggs, Katherine, *A Dictionary of British Folktales*, Routledge

Crossley-Holland, Kevin, *The Dead Moon*, André Deutsch

Crossley-Holland, Kevin, *The Norse Myths*, André Deutsch

Dahl, Louis H., *The Roman Camp and the Irish Saint*, Jarrold & Sons

Davies, Owen, *Cunning Folk*, Hambledon & London

Dixon, G. M., *Folktales and Legends of Norfolk*, Minimax Books

Downing & Millman, *Civil War*, Parkgate Books

Elliott, Colin, *Steam Fishermen in Old Photographs*, Tops'l Books

Elphick, Peter, *Out of Norfolk: Seamen & Travellers*, Orlando Publishing

Evans, George Ewart, *The Crooked Scythe*, Faber

Friedman, Jerome, *Miracles and the Pulp Press During the English Revolution*, UCL Press

Geoffrey of Monmouth, *History of the Kings of Britain*, Penguin

Glyde, John, *Folklore and Customs of Norfolk*, EP Publishing Ltd

Holmes, Neil, *The Lawless Coast*, Larks Press

Houghton, Bryan, *Saint Edmund, King and Martyr*, Terence Dalton Ltd

Howat, Polly, *Norfolk Ghosts and Legends*, Countryside Books

James, M. R., *Suffolk and Norfolk*, J. M. Dent & Sons

Jones, Trefor, *The English Saints*, Canterbury Press
Keane, John, *Tom Paine: A Political Life*, Bloomsbury
Ketton-Cremer, R.W., *Norfolk in the Civil War*, Faber
Knyvet Wilson, B., *Norfolk Tales and Memories*, Jarrold & Sons
Lambert & Gray, *Kings and Queens*, Collins
Le Strange, Richard, *Monasteries of Norfolk*, Yates Publishing
Lynch, Patricia, *Knights of God*, Bodley Head
Mackie, C., *Norfolk Annals Vol. 1 & 2*, Norfolk Chronicle
MacKillop, James, *Dictionary of Celtic Mythology*, Oxford University Press
Pevsner, N., *The Buildings of England (Norfolk)*, Penguin
Phillip, Neil, *English Folktales*, Penguin
Phillips, Rev. Fr. Andrew, *The Hallowing of England*, Anglo-Saxon Books
Porter, Enid, *The Folklore of East Anglia*, Batsford
Rackham, Oliver, *The History of the Countryside*, Phoenix
Rainbird Clarke, R., *East Anglia*, Thames & Hudson
Readers Digest Association, *Folklore, Myths and Legends of Britain*, Readers Digest
Reeve, Christopher, *A Straunge and Terrible Wonder*, Morrow
Roberts, Bob, *Last of the Sailormen*, R. & K. Paul
Robinson, Bruce, *Norfolk Mysteries Revisited*, Elmstead Publications
Ross, Anne & Robins, Don, *The Life & Death of a Druid Prince*, Rider
Rye, Walter, *Recreations of a Norfolk Antiquary*, Holt
Rye, Walter, *Tourist's Guide to the County of Norfolk*, Pickard Press
Sampson, C., *Ghosts of the Broads*, Yachtsman Publishing Co.
Sebald, W.G., *The Rings of Saturn*, Vintage
Simms, Nicholas, *The Footfall's Echo*, Orlando Publishing
Skelton, John, *The Complete English Poems*, Penguin
Storey, Neil, *The Little Book of Norfolk*, The History Press
Taylor, Richard, *How to Read a Church*, Rider
Tennyson, Julian, *Suffolk Scene*, Blackie & Son
Tongue, Ruth, *Forgotten Folk-tales of the English Counties*, R. & K. Paul
Trevelyan, G.M., *Illustrated History of England*, Longmans
Westwood, Jennifer, *Gothick Norfolk*, Shire Publications
Westwood, Jennifer, *Albion*, Granada
Westwood, Jennifer & Simpson, Jaqueline, *The Lore of the Land*, Penguin

WEBSITES

bbc.co.uk/history
British History Online (british-history.ac.uk)
East Anglian Traditional Music Trust (eatmt.org)
English Broadside Ballad Archive (ebba.english.ucsb.edu)
Googlebooks
Gutenberg.org
Hidden East Anglia (hiddenea.com)
Urbanlegends.about.com
Wikipedia

218820UK00001B/21/P